An Introduction to Data Base Design

Wiley Business Data Processing Library

Editors: **Richard G. Canning and J. Daniel Couger**

Personnel Implications for Business Data Processing
Robert A. Dickmann

Design of Sequential File Systems
Thomas R. Gildersleeve

Management Reporting Systems
James M. McKeever in collaboration with Benedict Kruse

A Guide to Packaged Systems
Robert V. Head

Control of the Information System Development Cycle
Robert I. Benjamin

Decision Tables: Theory and Practice
Solomon L. Pollack, Harry T. Hicks, Jr., and William J. Harrison

An Introduction to Data Base Design
John K. Lyon

The Organization of the Data Processing Function
Frederic G. Withington

An Introduction to Data Base Design

John K. Lyon

Honeywell Information Systems, Inc.
Schenectady, New York

Wiley-Interscience

a Division of John Wiley & Sons, Inc.
New York • London • Sydney • Toronto

Library of Congress Catalogue Card Number: 75-155904

ISBN 0 471 55735 8 (cloth) ISBN 0 471 55739 0 (paper)

Printed in the United States of America.

10 9 8 7 6 5 4

Library Editors' Preface

The *Wiley Business Data Processing Library* is intended for professionals and for persons desiring to improve their competence in business/management applications of the computer. Within each of some twenty subject areas, publications will be provided over a range of technical depth. The objective is a series of publications that enable readers to gain an understanding in specialized subject areas.

The Library is designed to offer succinct treatment of specialized subjects, allowing many authorities in the computer field to participate as authors.

The Library is designed to cover three levels of interest for detailed technical information:

One-Star Titles. For those in the field and others who want to gain background information about the subject: data processing managers and business programmers and analysts.

Two-Star Titles. For those who have some experience in this subject and who wish to study the more technical aspects of it: data processing managers and business programmers and analysts.

Three-Star Titles. For those with extensive experience who want a highly technical discussion: data processing managers, senior business programmers and analysts.

The increase in breadth, complexity, and the dynamic characteristics of the computer field make a Library such as this imperative—for training and for reference. The breadth is illustrated by the many subject areas covered in the Library: from data base design to business planning by way of simulation; from hardware-software evaluation and selection to personnel considerations for business data processing. The growth of complexity is apparent in each of these subject areas; for instance, the variations in data base design and data management systems are increasing almost weekly. The dynamics of the field are obvious, with the multitude of new hardware and software products reaching the market each year.

In the face of this growth in depth and complexity, practitioners encounter the problems of developing and maintaining technical competence. The novice must upgrade his competence to reach the experienced practitioner level. The experienced system analyst and programmer must strive to reach senior levels. The professional must broaden his knowledge to include new specialties that adjoin his areas of technical competence.

Training, updating, and upgrading professionals in the computer field will be a continuous problem. We hope that the Library will be an effective method in helping to cope with this problem.

RICHARD G. CANNING
J. DANIEL COUGER
Library Editors

Preface

At any gathering of "computer" people, mention of the term "data base" is sufficient to evoke a full range of responses from skepticism of the cynic, the fervent support of some particular proprietary offering, to the unspoiled enthusiasm of the uninitiated. The term "data base" does not have a single accepted definition. As normally used today, a data base is whatever the designer chooses to call a data base. I hope that the first several sections of this communigraph will serve to provide a more objective image of a data base.

This communigraph has been written for the programmer, analyst, or designer who is aware of the limitations of conventional techniques for storing, retrieving, and processing information, is motivated to tap the potential of a data base, and is confronted with the challenge of applying now the techniques of data base design.

These techniques are manufacturer, machine, and device independent; unfortunately, the ease with which any given design can be implemented is manufacturer, machine, and device dependent.

While the various immediate access storage (IAS) devices such as disk, drum, and CRAM, have accelerated the development and implementation of data base design techniques, they are also useful in the design of tape-oriented systems. The concepts and methods described in this communigraph are intended to introduce, through discussion and example, the process of design from initial inception through final implementation.

The discussions of knotted list (threaded list) processors should provide a useful insight into the capabilities of the emerging manufacturer supplied software and the evolving data base language under consideration by the Data Base Task Group of CODASYL. The techniques described in this communigraph have, in varying degrees, been developed, evaluated, and extended during the last six years using a variety of equipment and in applications which include the following:

- Manufacturing
- Resource allocation
- Inventory control
- Order entry
- General accounting
- Project control
- Defense intelligence
- Warehouse and distribution analysis
- Selective dissemination of information

While each application is characterized by its own distinctive elements, they also contain common elements and illustrate the importance of modeling as part of the process of designing a data base.

I thank my wife who typed and proofread the manuscript and Bill Helgeson who introduced me to the world of data bases and must have struggled (perhaps even shuddered) during my education under his tutelage.

JOHN K. LYON

Schenectady, New York
January 1971

Contents

An Introduction to Data Base Design

SECTION 1

Overview–The Data Base

The data base and its continually evolving technology are providing the user, analyst, and programmer with the capability to challenge the true information processing potential of the digital computer. This section presents a definition of a data base, free from commercial attachments, and its role in information processing. Having established such a definition and the relationship to fields, records, and files, the role of, and necessity for, the design process during the development of a data base is examined. The importance of physical and logical structure is discussed as a preview to the remaining sections. Finally, this section outlines, in broad terms, the structure and objectives of the communigraph, and its intended value at each experience level.

THE DATA BASE

"Base" is defined as follows:

- The bottom of anything, considered as its support or foundation.
- The fundamental part of a thing.
- The chief ingredient of anything, viewed as its fundamental constituent.
- Mathematically, the number with reference to which a mathematical table is constructed.
- A point or line from which a start is made.
- Base in its most general sense equals bottom but, more specifically, implies a broad bottom by which something is held up or stabilized.

Each of these six definitions provides some insight into the nature of a data base. The first three emphasize the importance of the data base as the fundamental element and, simultaneously, as the foundation upon which something else will be built.

For our purpose the "something else" is information. Webster defines information as: "knowledge derived from . . . observation . . . ; especially from unorganized facts or data." Since the sole purpose of a data base is to facilitate the production of information, it should never be considered as an end in itself, but rather as the foundation for information. Analysis and logical organization of data are part of the process by which knowledge is derived.

The fourth and fifth definitions represent a philosophical outlook to the designer of data bases. Namely, a data base is the starting point from which all information processes are constructed. This concept of the data base as the starting point is elemental to the design process and is the subject of the second section.

The last definition, while not emphasizing the concept of a starting point, is an equally important concept; namely, the data base must be broad enough, not only to support an information process, but also to stabilize it. The data base, in other words, must provide sufficient breadth to permit an information process to "weather the storms of change." If a process or system is to survive, it must be built upon a solid foundation.

This view of a data base is in direct contrast to the pyramid philosophy of system design which views a data base as a triangle (see Figure 1-1). The establishment of a triangular arrangement of data is based erroneously on the naive belief that it is possible to anticipate the needs of top and middle level management. It is even more naive to believe that it is possible to anticipate their desires. Unfortunately, the success of a system is not measured by how well it fulfills needs, but rather how well it fulfills desires.

While the pyramid implies that top management sits directly in the middle of the functional spectrum of business, managers always view business in terms of their dominant functional background; for example, a salesman will always view the business in terms of orders received; the finance man, in terms of the general ledger account; the

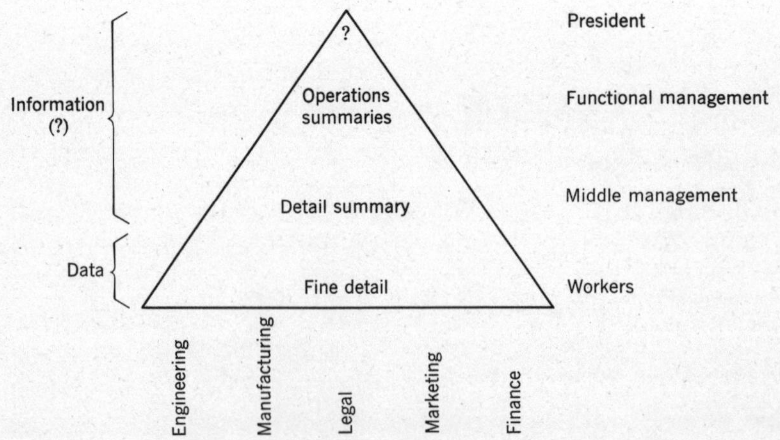

Figure 1-1 **Pyramidal organization of data.**

engineer, in terms of a better "widget"; and finally, the manufacturing man, in terms of units shipped. It is only natural to analyze a problem not only in the total context but also in terms of those details which are most familiar.

If an information system is built on a "triangular base," ultimately it will serve no one. If the triangle is biased toward the functional background of the current top management, it will hinder rather than serve the business at a time when information is needed most; namely, when management changes. Assuming that such a rigid system would be tolerated in the first place, the game of "management musical chairs" leads to job security for the information processing staff—they can never catch up.

The intent of a triangular structure is to provide all levels of management with the depth of detail which they need and desire. This detail must be information and not data. Since information is knowledge derived from data, then it follows that the data do not have a triangular structure, but rather, that the processing of the data yields information suitable to the user. Recognizing that management turnover is a fact, it is only logical to provide a data base which is broad enough to cover the desires of any management, and which leaves the "tailoring" of information to the process.

As a matter of fact, the data which describe a company and its relationship to its environment is essentially independent of management. It is only the information that is produced from the data base that reflects the personality of management.

THE NATURE OF DATA

Datum is "something, actual or assumed, used as a basis of reckoning." Immediately, the terms

- Something
- Assumed or actual
- Used
- Basis of reckoning

stand out—they describe the nature of data.

First, the fact that datum is "something" implies that it can be identified and described. It is not necessarily physical in terms of the measurable world, but may also be intangible or purely logical.

Second, datum may be either assumed or real. Thus a data base is not limited to facts but may also include

- Forecasts
- Wild guesses
- Assumptions
- Sales reports, and so on

Third, datum is used. This is the most difficult property to cope with in the design of a data base. How does a designer decide what will be used in the future, and then, at what level of detail will it be maintained? In fact, the "use" property of data may be the true topic of this communigraph. It is extremely important that "use" not be abused by limiting the data base to current usage, but rather that "use" be determined by the existence of a logical relationship to other things and hence its potential usage. If use is restricted in the data base, either structurally or procedurally, then the stabilizing effects of a data base are jeopardized. Structural restrictions result, for example, by limiting the number of occurrences, such as allowing only one field for wife's name in an employee record. Procedural restrictions, on the other hand, are typically placed on the use of data by summarization (e.g., carrying year-to-date total instead of the 12 monthly values).

Finally, datum is the basis for reckoning, the elemental quantity used to produce knowledge. This final aspect of the nature of data can also be legitimately construed to imply that the contents of the data base are pertinent to the production of information. The amount and type of "data" to be incorporated in a data base must reflect the information needs of the business. The primary distinction between "use" and "basis for reckoning" is one of potential versus current use. "Basis for reckoning" determines physically the current contents of the data base. "Use" determines logically the kinds of data which are, or could be, contained in the data base. "Use" is the logical design of the base while "basis for reckoning" is the current physical content. It is imperative that the logical and implementation designs always be compatible.

THE STORAGE OF DATA

Data are stored physically on and in a myriad of devices. Some can be directly computer-processed while others must be converted prior to processing. Regardless of the device or media used to store data, the hierarchical concept of

- Files
- Records
- Fields

is almost universally accepted, at least to the record level. The concept of a field is generally accepted in the realm of electronic data processing, but, for a variety of reasons, it may elude the non-edp user. Webster fails to cope with the concept of a "field," but by deduction, we can achieve a satisfactory definition. A file is a logical, defined collection of records. It is logical in the sense that the originator of the file defined, perhaps arbitrarily, the property of membership in the file for each of the records. Furthermore, the logical limits of the file membership are defined. Physical membership, that is, records actually in the file, is less than, or equal to, the logical membership of the file. In other words, it is possible for a record that may exist logically in the file to be absent physically. This concept of a file is valid and acceptable whether or not the file is computer readable. The primary distinction between paper and computer files is the ease with which logical membership is altered; the membership of a paper file is obviously much easier to change than the membership of a computer file, if for no other reason than that the discipline of a paper file is less rigid.

A record is a logical, defined collection of fields. As such, what constitutes a field and a record is the arbitrary prerogative of the person making the definition. It is completely possible that one person may define a file folder within a paper file as a "record" and each piece of correspondence within the folder as a field. The same file when viewed by another person may result in the definition of each piece of correspondence within a folder as a separate record, each with its own set of fields. Perhaps a more appropriate analogy is the pay record of an employee which is maintained on a preprinted form. Each element or block within the form represents a field. The field, for our purposes, represents an element of data—fact or assumption—which is pertinent to the business. The total collection of data—the data base—is, in fact, the quantitative and qualitative description of the business. The data base is one or more files which may or may not be machine readable. In later sections, additional logical significance will be given to files, records, and fields.

Physically, a file is associated with a device or media (disk unit, magnetic tape, a filing cabinet) implying addressability. It should be obvious that

- A logical file may extend across more than one physical file.

- A physical file may contain all, or parts, of more than one logical file.

Just as a physical file implies addressability, a physical record implies a unit of transfer. In the case of the preprinted form of the pay record, the physical record is a minimum quanta for transfer—you get all of it whether or not you want it. A physical record may contain

- One or more logical records
- One or more different kinds of logical records

At the same time it is conceivable that a logical record may reside within one or more physical records.

The field, or data element, becomes the quanta of logical comprehension. It is the field that is the basis of knowledge; it is the field that supports analysis; it is the field that permits comparison and examination.

It is paramount that the designer clearly define and maintain the distinction between the physical world of data bases (files, records, and fields) and the corresponding logical world.

It is unfortunate that the disagreement which exists today, concerning the role and definition of the data base in information processing, is due almost entirely to the failure to separate physical and logical concepts. The academic and research communities are tempted to ignore the physical, while the hardware salesman is prone to ignore the logical. The momentary stance of any given manufacturer of processors and peripherals or suppliers of software can be traced directly to their ability or inability to accommodate both worlds.

COMING ATTRACTIONS

The remaining sections will attempt to establish and illustrate the role of the logical and physical aspects of data bases and the interaction between them. A strong emphasis has been placed on the design process itself. Wherever possible, examples of specific logical and physical structures will be explored in light of "why each has chosen" and "what were the basic alternatives?" The following sections have been laid out in an attempt to lead the reader step-by-step to a logical approach to data base design.

Each section in the communigraph is organized to take advantage of the preceding sections and to establish the foundation for those that follow. For the newcomer to the world of data base technology, this should provide the desired rate of exposure to permit an understanding and appreciation of the potential of a data base. At the same time, some warning of the possible hazards are presented. For the old timer, the progression from one topic to another hopefully will permit some insight into why some designs fail and others succeed. The communigraph is intended to stimulate the reader to relate his own experience to the thoughts expressed in each section.

The order of development of each topic is to examine the moderately theoretical basis and then to relate it to examples. Such an approach is intended to show that there is more science than art to the design of data bases. The data base design process, while not an exact science, is based on a concept of a logical design which is then reduced to practice as an implementation. Along the way, the techniques of modeling, communicating, and inducing efficiency are discussed. Finally, in the last section, four data bases are discussed in light of alternatives, user objectives, and primary aspects of its resulting performance.

The techniques and structures discussed are biased toward the newer data management languages currently available or under development by the various manufacturers. It is particularly applicable to the capabilities of the language specified by the

CODASYL data base task group. This language has been recommended by the DBTG as the standard for an extension to Cobol. Regardless of the language or technique used to implement a data base, the logical design process is essentially the same.

SECTION 2

Logical Organization– The Basis for Structure

Regardless of the intent of any design endeavor, it is desirable to examine systematically the purpose, salient techniques, measurable parameters (input), and desired results (output) of a specific application. This section concentrates on the necessity for logical organization of data and its relationship to the input, output, and internal processing. The process of establishing relationships is introduced by presenting the main types of file organization and the logical advantages and disadvantages of each. Specifically, this section treats serial, inverted, list, and threaded list structures. While treated in greater detail in Section 5, the more common techniques for implementing these logical structures and concise examples of each structural type are presented.

DESIGN APPROACH

While there are many variations in the approaches used during the design of an information system, they may be classified as either file or process-oriented. This distinction may appear frivolous, but the ability of a system to adapt to change is the result of its design. In order to illustrate clearly the distinction between a process and file-oriented design consider, briefly, a payroll system. A payroll system is intended to pay people, fulfill the associated statutory reporting requirements, generate management reports, and, in some cases, supply information needed for personnel and salary administration.

The process-oriented designer tends to initiate design by identifying and defining each of the system-run units in terms of internal processing, leading to a determination of the data required by each program. Finally, after each "process" unit is defined, the designer reviews his data requirements and constructs a file. This approach yields suboptimization; that is, relatively efficient programs but with repeated intermediate sorts and/or merges of files. A process-oriented design concentrates on the processing of a single program or subsystem, and therefore tends to resist changing requirements; that is, the programs are too procedurally bound to the environment of the moment. This resistance to change is evidenced by

- Excessive cost and/or time to incorporate program changes
- Proliferation of ''master'' files and/or sorts
- Demise of valid documentation as the number of patches exceeds original code
- Six or seven different sets of octal patch cards in the pocket of each programmer

The alternative to process orientation is a design which begins by an examination of the total system in terms of information. A file-oriented designer would look at the payroll problem in terms of things, values, relationships, and, finally, processes. The file approach defines the information elements of a system and then organizes them such that the information remains valid even though the details of the process change. A system based on information content will survive changing requirements and in many cases the design will encourage extensions.

THE PAYROLL EXAMPLE

Process Orientation

In examining various elements of a payroll system, several typical processes can be identified, namely:

- Entry and editing of time and piecework vouchers
- Compensation computation
- Payroll distribution
- Check processing
- Maintenance
- Management reporting
- Statutory reporting

Each of these typical run units require and, in turn, produce different kinds of information, usually in competing format and sequence. The processing of a labor voucher requires the availability of the following elements: pay number, incentives, benefit data, and/or overtime validation data. On the other hand, compensation computation requires access to hours and rates, incentives (pieces and rates), residence and/or tax codes, numbers of dependents, tax limits, tax tables, exception tables, and so on.

The designer has at his disposal many different techniques for accessing, processing, and retaining the data necessary for each specific process. It is only natural that the selection of technique, form, and sequence of data will be biased by the requirements of each individual program and thus tend to be tied to each run unit. This tendency to optimize the "data form" for each run unit is responsible for any proliferation of files and sorts and the system's inability to gracefully survive change.

FILE ORIENTATION

The payroll problem, as viewed by the file-oriented designer, contains the same elements as those of his process-oriented contemporary, but with a shift in emphasis. The file designer attempts to define the information elements which are basic to payroll and to identify the significant relationships among them; specifically, the central element of a payroll system is the employee, or more appropriately, a person. A person may be identified by a Social Security number, employee number, and name, and is described by

- Rates and pay, past and present
- Incentive eligibility, past and present
- Job classifications, past and present
- Cost/work center assignment, past and present
- Skills
- Dependents
- Benefit participation and eligibility, past and present
- Tax rates, liability, limits, and payments
- Personal descriptive data: education, training, birthdate, service date, and so on

In addition to the person, a payroll system contains other significant and identifiable information elements. One of the most obvious is the "organization," or the administrative cost center. An organization is identified by its name and, normally, a code number and is described by its mission, responsibility, and relationships to other organizations. An organization may be a work center, cost center, administrative center, plant, or even the company itself.

An obvious logical relationship exists between the two types or kinds of things that have been identified; namely, people and organizations. The first of these relationships is one of ownership or, in other words, one of assignment. Each employee is assigned administratively to one, and only one, organization. This relationship is, in fact, stronger than mere assignment; namely, an employee must be assigned administratively to one organization. If an employee has been transferred between groups, another relationship, **previous assignment**,* may be indicated. Note that while an employee must be assigned to one group administratively, he may be related to none, one, two, or any number of prior organizations; the number of assignments is the only limit. Also, it is logically possible for a person to have been assigned more than once to the same organization. The data base structure should accommodate both situations. Additionally, a nonadministrative relationship can be identified, recognizing, for example, that people may perform work for organizations to which they are not administratively assigned. The association of the manager, a **person**, with the organization is yet another example of a logical relationship between different kinds of entities.

The file-oriented designer concentrates on the basic information element of the system—the person—and will design the file such that it establishes and maintains the logical integrity of the **person**, the subsidiary information elements, and finally the relationships among the elements. Information elements and relationships may be implemented either as separate records or as fields within a record. Having logically defined the information content of the system, the designer then proceeds to design each of the required run units around the complete file. Because the file is not tailored to each specific run unit, the system will be flexible enough to accommodate changes in any of the individual run units. Experience has shown that systems, which are designed in this manner, tend to have programs which are interpretive and, as such, are capable of accommodating without alteration changes in the amount and form of the data in the

* Terms in boldface refer to the class or set of similar "things." An individual member of a set may be referred to by the same term, but will not be in boldface. For example, a single person belongs to the set or class **person**.

single "master file." It is also possible, with such systems, to add, change, or delete programs without drastically disrupting the other programs in the system.

Hopefully, these simple, but contrasting, views of a payroll system are useful in illustrating the distinction between process and file-oriented system design. As systems have become more comprehensive and complex, the file-oriented design approach has proved repeatedly its capability to successfully cope with continually, changing system requirements. As this trend toward integration of systems continues, it is imperative that the primary focus for the design effort be on the information content of the system rather than on the processes.

INFORMATION SPACE

In the preceding subsection, two kinds of things were important to the discussion of the logical design of an information system—"things" and "relationships" between or among "things." This section dwells upon "things"; the role of "relationships" is discussed in the next section.

Two different kinds of things, **persons** and **organizations**, were discussed within the context of the payroll file. These things or entities are commonly represented within a file as records. Entities, in the real world, possess certain properties which distinguish them, uniquely, from all other entities. These distinguishing properties are identifiers. A Social Security number, for example, in a payroll application may be used as an identifier for a person. Entities possess other properties, known as descriptors, which may uniquely identify them. Within the payroll example, an employee's salary, name, age, and so on were descriptors of a person. An identifier is, in fact, a unique descriptor.

Within a file, descriptors are normally represented by fields within a record or by an association with other records. For example, a Social Security number would be a field in the **person** record. However, the descriptor which identifies the organization of assignment may very well be established by the association of a person with the appropriate **organization** record. This latter case, that is, description by association, is actually an example of redefining an entity to serve as a descriptor. In fact, the **organization** record in the payroll system is an entity in its own right and at the same time a descriptor by association of the **person** record.

Information can be completely described in terms of three elements:

- Entities
- Attributes
- Values

Examined in the light of the Information Triplet, any object (entity) is completely defined in terms of attributes and the associated values. Note that a descriptor is a specific attribute/value pair. For example, if the neighbor's car is described as a red Ford, a known entity (the neighbor's car) is being described in terms of its descriptors or in terms of its attribute/value pairs.

Attribute	Value
Color	Red
Manufacturer	Ford
Owner	Neighbor
Class of "Thing"	Car

Imagine a three-dimensional orthogonal space with one axis labeled **Attribute**; then, for the car described above, there is a plane for the attribute color which is parallel to the other two axes (**value** and **entity**), as shown in Figure 2-1. Thus any descriptor involving **color** lies somewhere in the **"color"** plane. In similar fashion, the value "red" describes a plane which is parallel to the **attribute** and **entity** axes (Figure 2-2). Thus

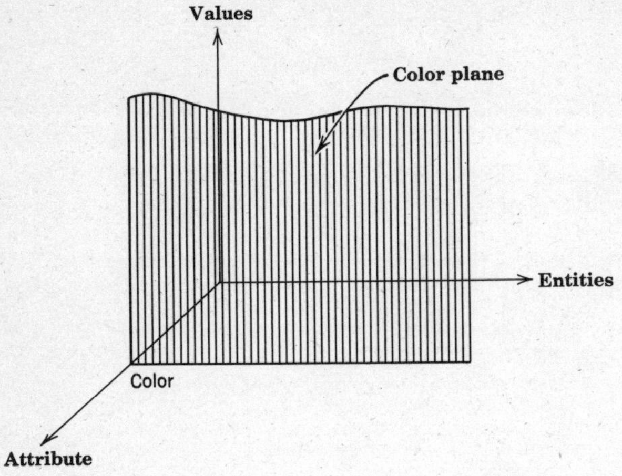

Figure 2-1 **The "plane" for the attribute color.**

all descriptors with the value red must lie somewhere on this plane. Note, that the value red applies to all attributes, not just **color**, for example, the attribute **political outlook**. The straight line which is defined by the intersection of the planes for a given **value** and **attribute** is a specific descriptor,

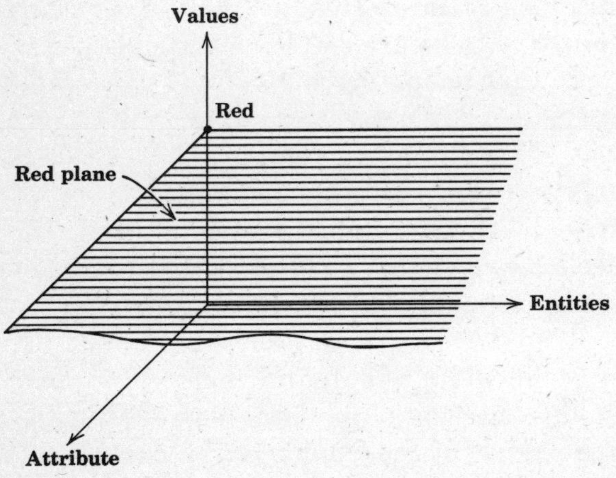

Figure 2-2 **The "plane" for the value red.**

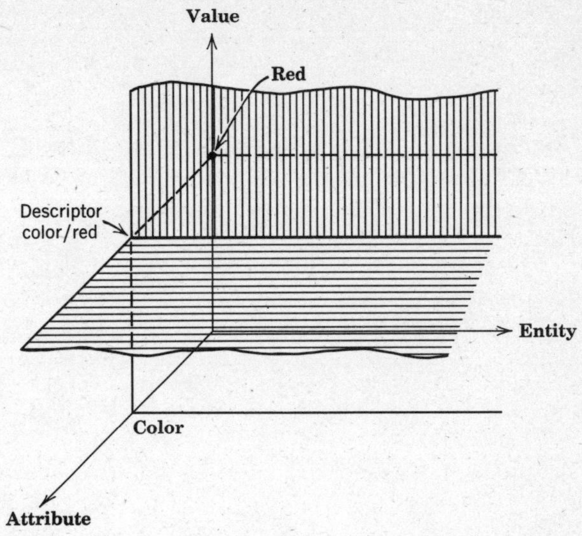

Figure 2-3 **The "line" for the descriptor Color/Red.**

for example, **color/red** (Figure 2-3). In fact, the general term **"descriptor"** is the intersection of any **value** and **attribute** plane.

The third dimension of this conceptual information space is that of the **entity.** For a given, and therefore each, entity (such as the neighbor's car) there is a plane parallel to the other two axes. Therefore it follows that any descriptor which applies to a given entity is represented by a point defined by the intersection of the **entity** plane and the **descriptor** line as in Figure 2-4. An information element is therefore the intersection of the three planes; that is, it is uniquely defined in terms of specific:

- Attribute
- Value
- Entity

For the example of the neighbor's car, four distinct information elements were defined. All four of these elements lie in the common plane defined by the **entity**—the neighbor's car.

Within the context of the three-dimen-

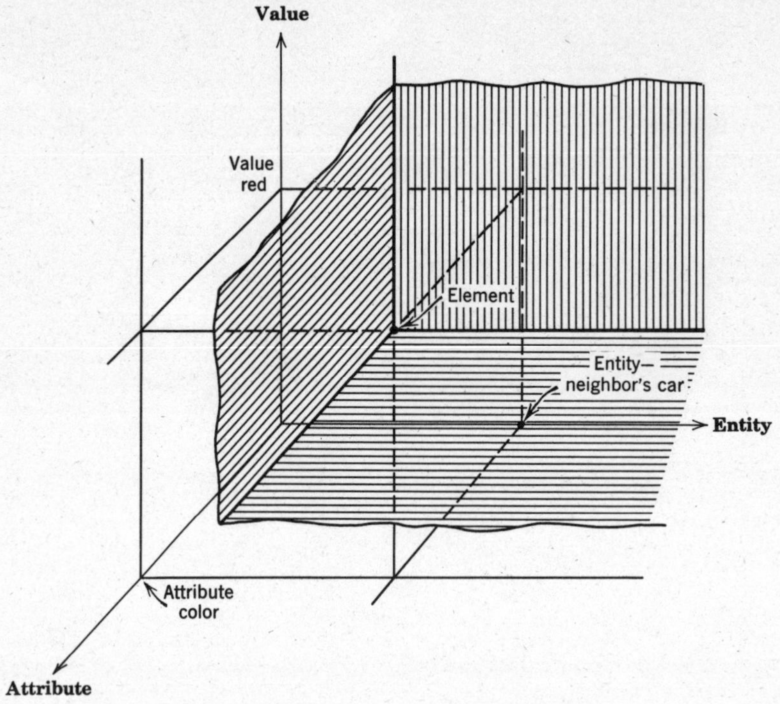

Figure 2-4 **The information element—neighbor's red car.**

sional information space, each axis represents an elemental information class. All of the properties of an **entity,** its **descriptors,** are found within the plane of the **entity.** The existence or presence of a given **descriptor** may be thought of as a node or a point. The "location" of this information node is given by the (**entity, attribute, value**) coordinates. Data base design is the process of defining a subset of the total information space and the creation of convenient paths between the elements of the subset.

The data base designer defines what kind and how many of each entity, attribute, and value will be permitted to exist within that portion of the "total" information space represented by his data base. Each data base represents a subspace. As a practical matter, the designer of the payroll system recognizes implicitly that while he is interested in people (an entity class) he is specifically interested in only those people (entities) who are employees. He also recognizes that people have many descriptors but that he needs access to only a limited number. By defining an **"employee"** record, the class of entity is admitted to this new subspace with the implied restriction that each occurrence of this kind of record represents a person employed by the firm.

The designer now proceeds to bound his space in the attribute dimension by defining fields which will be contained within each occurrence of the **"employee"** record; for example, Social Security number, name, address, age, and rate of pay. Each attribute (field name) represents a plane in both the total information space and the subspace represented by the data base. The purpose of defining the subspace (data base) by limiting the number of attributes, value, and entity types is to reduce physical space requirements and to minimize access to data.

In the total space, the descriptors for a particular entity are located by searching the entire plane for that entity. Theoretically, this plane is essentially unlimited in both dimensions (there are an essentially unlimited number of **attributes** and **values** available). The process of defining fields (**attributes**) existing within a type of record is analogous to establishing a finite (even short) path to all **attributes** of interest. Physically these **attributes** are immediately known or addressable by virtue of definition.

Each occurrence of the employee record then defines several nodes or points within the total space. Namely, each record corresponds to a separate point on the **entity** axis and each field to a separate point on the **attribute** axis, and finally, the values of these fields in each of the occurrences (i.e., each employee) of the records represent points or positions along the **value** axis. Note that there is a 1–1 relationship between the number of records physically present and the number of "points" along the **entity** axis. The number of **attributes** is independent of the number of fields defined. The number of specific values is proportional to the number of fields and records; specifically, it will be less than or equal to the product of the number of fields and records.

For example, the payroll system defined two classes or sets of entities: **person** and **organization.** This is precisely a definition of two subsets of the entire space. In this case the subsets are mutually exclusive and the implied linear transformations are independent. However, when the dependence/ownership association between these two **entity** sets is established, they are no longer independent. Specifically, two classes of entities from the information space are being mapped into a smaller space (the data base) such that the members of the subset **person** cannot exist unless the owning member of the **organization** subset also exists. This does not mean that a member of the **person** subset cannot be referenced uniquely without reference to the owning **organization,** but, rather, that they cannot exist unless the owning **organization** exists. It does mean, however, that a **person** can also be referenced by way of the owning **organization.**

Each relationship, whether one of dependence or equivalence, is a mapping from one subset of the information space to another. Because they are mappings, it is desirable to ensure that each of the **entity** sets is mutually exclusive, if for no other reason than to avoid ambiguity. This results when a single value in one space can give multiple values in another. This by itself is not dangerous unless a single value can lead to inconsistent results if different paths are taken. For example, it is hoped that the organization obtained, if accessed via a person, would have a path leading back to the same person. It is the designer's task to ensure that this type of integrity will exist within the data base, either through the logical structure of the data base or through the discipline imposed by the programs.

How does this relate to file design? Simply by providing a basic understanding of data and information. All current memory and file devices are one dimensional. We have just shown that information is, at a minimum, three dimensional. A typical payroll file may be sorted by Social Security number—each number identifying an entity, the employee. The process of reading the file, in sequence, is equivalent to starting at the origin and "walking" the length of the **entity** axis. If a nine-digit Social Security number is used to identify uniquely each employee, all possible **values** are not present in the file—only those values of the actual employees. This is equivalent to mapping a subset (**employees**) of all people with a Social Security number.

If the concept of a basic, three-dimensional information space is accepted, one can expect to be able to process in any single dimension or along any defined path (i.e., in two dimensions). This means that in the dimension **attribute,** a specific attribute, that is, color, could be scanned to determine all current values and to identify the entities which possess the attribute color. Furthermore, it implies that the designer can describe any path by defining a transformation of the space of any subset into any other meaningful space.

If the records in a sequential file contain a field which represents the attribute color, the dimensional processing discussed above is equivalent to reading the file from end to end and examining each record in turn. This is obviously a tedious and expensive task with a large file. If the file is sorted with the color field as the key (i.e., placed in **value** sequence for the attribute color), the file is said to be inverted on **color.** Note that the attribute **color** can have multiple values for any one person:

- Hair color
- Eye color
- Skin color

As a matter of fact, there is no reason to restrict any given entity to a fixed number of values for a given attribute. In a single record-type file, each record represents an entity. The fields within the record usually represent **descriptors.** In the payroll file, how many fields should be included for the descriptor **dependent name?** There could be a need for as few as zero or as many as *n* occurrences. On the other hand, since it is an identifier, the descriptor Social Security number occurs exactly once. Note that a field name represents an attribute while each occurrence of a field is a descriptor, that is, an attribute/value pair.

This concept of information space may also be of assistance in a purely physical sense when considering the effects of redundant data. The "total" space permits each **entity, value,** and **attribute** to exist only once. Note as in the discussion of the effect of defining a data base in terms of records and fields that each definition of a field within a record is permitting repeated values to exist. For example a field (Attribute) representing **sex** in an Employee record can have at most two values, male or female. Thus each occurrence of an employee record (after the first of each kind) introduces redundant data. While this is an extreme case, it does illustrate the point.

The file-oriented designer concerns himself with the definition of his own information space. The goal of his design effort is a space with a minimum of redundancy in dimensions but with enough paths between subsets to encourage efficient processing. As a minimum, he is attempting to define a space which is sufficient to describe conveniently every entity or combination of entities which the system can encounter.

SECTION 3

Graphical Notation–The Basis for Communication

According to a great Chinese philosopher and programmer, a flow chart is worth at least three source decks; in addition, it is obviously true that the most elaborately designed data base is, at best, only an intellectual exercise if there is no basis for communicating its properties. This section introduces a graphical notation for describing logical organization, that is, the structure of a data base.

This notation has been in use for several years and has proven its capability to communicate accurately and adequately the structure of many different data bases. While we may not all agree with a particular data base design, the structure diagram permits each of the protagonists to select explicitly their points of disagreement.

The notation for the two basic elements of any data base structure, the **record** and the **association,** are introduced. Using these two elements, the elementary forms are described. A series of examples relate these basic forms to the more familiar structural representations: the list, table, and matrix. Specific implied and explicit logical existence criteria are presented (with examples) for each of the basic types.

THE STRUCTURE DIAGRAM

The structure diagram is a graphical representation of the logical organization of a data base. The diagram specifies the relationships of records within and between files, in much the same manner that a high-level program flow chart indicates the interaction of procedures. In many of the older information systems, the designer would create system segments which would operate on single record-type files. This is not to say that the systems operated only on a single record type; most required several "master" files and even more transaction or working files to complete the system flow. In these systems, the only documentation of file structure that existed were physical record and field layouts. Consequently, many of these systems have become virtually impossible to maintain. A single change in sort sequence or file layout can disrupt the entire system.

As more complex file structures are designed and implemented, the structure diagram is rapidly gaining acceptance. This is the direct result of the emergence of data base languages developed by the various users, user groups, and manufacturers.

The structure diagram is a logical representation of a file or data base. As flow charts and the file layout diagram are used to reflect the physical aspects of implementation, the structure diagram may indicate such things as number of characters, number of records, physical placement, sort sequence, access method.

The structure diagram is the medium for communication between designer and programmer. It is not only in the "Motherhood, God, and Country" category of documentation but is necessary to ensure successful parallel implementations of the various parts of a system. Specifically, it permits the parallel implementation of utility, maintenance, and application programs without mutual interference and frequent reprogramming.

STRUCTURE ELEMENTS

There are only two basic elements used to build a structure diagram. Graphically, these are the rectangle and the arrow. The rectangle indicates the existence of a group of "things" which are logically similar. In the terms of a file which contains five different types of records, the structure diagram would contain five different rectangles, one for each of the separate record types. At the outset, it is important to distinguish between the number of types of records and the total number of records.

The arrow is used to indicate the relationship between two or more types of records. This relationship is always one of membership or dependence. For example, if a payroll system had a file containing two kinds of records in it, namely, **employee** and **dependent** records, then the two record types are related (no pun intended) in a hierarchical sense. This is shown as

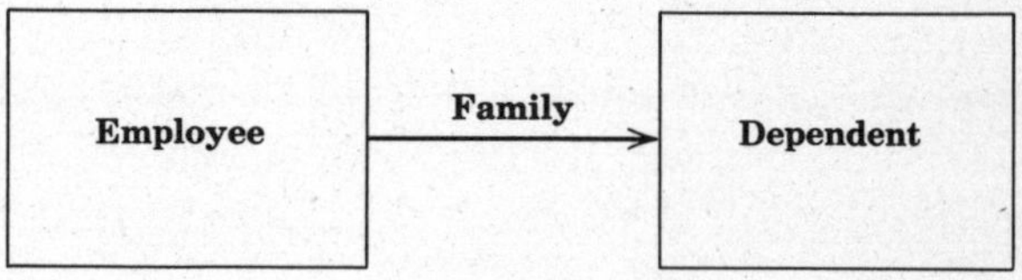

This diagram is interpreted as follows:

- Two, and only two, different kinds of things (entities) exist—**employees** and **dependents.**
- The **employee** and **dependent** are logically associated.
- An **employee** can "own" or be related to any number of **dependents**, that is, zero, one, two.
- A **dependent** must have one, and only one, **employee** as its "owner" in order to exist.

The arrow and each of the two rectangles represent collections of like things. The box labeled employee is used to define the existence of the class of things known as **employees.** The box labeled dependent not only defines the existence of a class of things known by that name but also indicates that the two classes, **dependent** and **employee,** are distinct. While the differences may be either logical or physical, they are significant enough to warrant distinction.

Things that possess differences in their own right may still be related in a logical sense. This relationship may be one of dependence as in the previous example; that is, the existence of a particular **dependent** depends on the existence of a specific employee who "owns" that dependent. The arrow also signifies commonality, that is, the dependents that belong to the same employee possess, in common, all of the properties and attributes of the employee.

In a slightly different connotation, the arrow represents the result of classification. In the example, the **dependent** is classified by **employee,** with the limitation that any one dependent cannot be classified simultaneously or related to more than one employee. The arrow represents exclusive sets.

Before going on to the next basic form, consider Figure 3-1. The top half represents five specific cases of the **employee/dependent** relationship including employee 8 with no dependents. Note that the case of a dependent without an employee is not shown since it is an inadmissible case, that is, a logical contradiction.

In terms of the previous section on information space, the rectangle represents a class of entities with each occurrence representing a specific "point" on the *Entity* axis. The arrow or relationship represents a path, starting at each owner entity and connecting (relating) each of the *dependent* entities. Thus if there were 10 employees, there would be 10 separate and distinct paths leading from each employee to each of *his* dependents. As in Figure 3-1 (employee 8), it is possible to have a null (empty) path. Note also that by our definition, an entity belonging to the **dependent** class cannot exist within the subspace of our data base unless it is contained in such a path.

The second basic structural form is used to indicate the relationship between two different and independent entities. For the purposes of illustration, consider the enti-

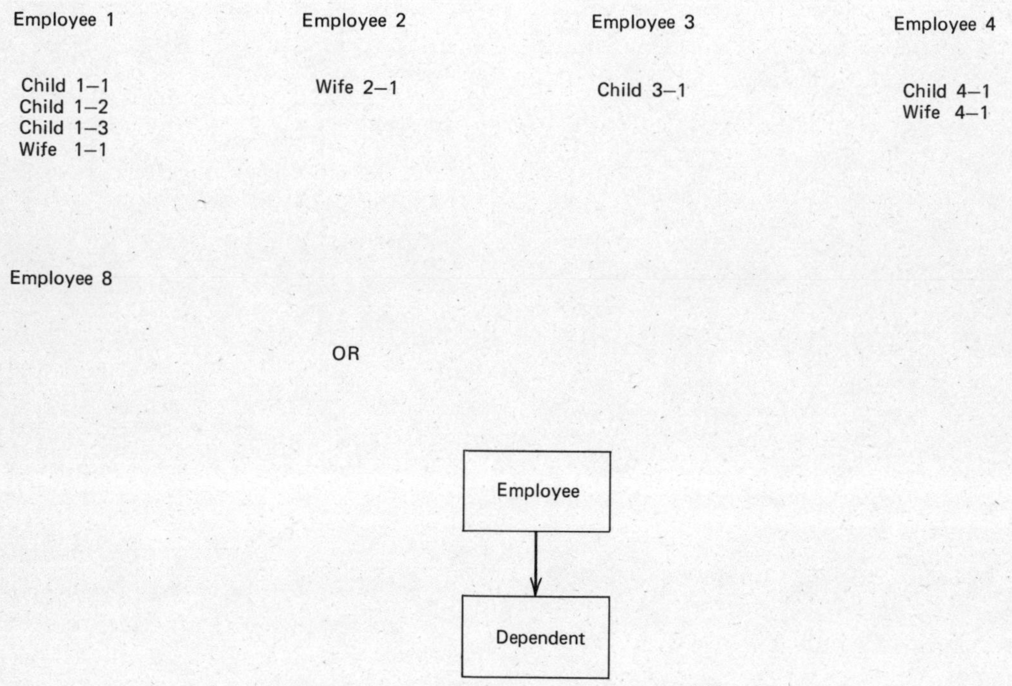

Figure 3-1 **Examples of the employee/dependent relationship.**

ties called **machine** and **employee.** We want to establish the existence of a relationship between the two, known as **skill.** Obviously, the existence of a machine in a factory does not depend upon the existence of a person who is skilled in its operation. Conversely, the existence of an employee in a factory does not depend on his ability to operate a machine—observe either the shop steward or the manager, depending upon your viewpoint. The two classes of things are obviously independent in the sense of existence, but at the same time a relationship can exist between them. This is shown as:

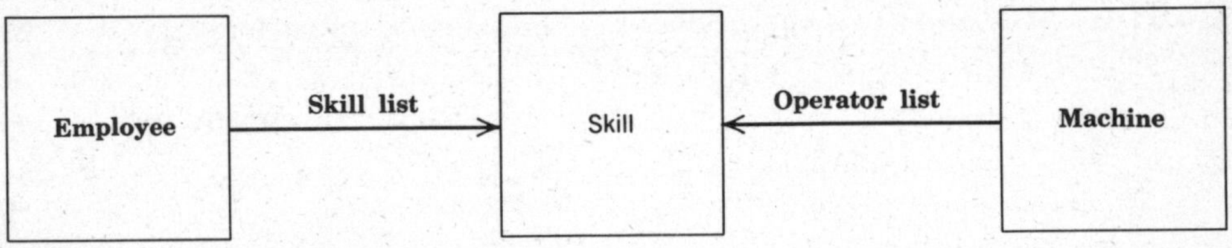

Specifically, a given skill cannot exist unless the owning employee and machine exist simultaneously. If the class of things called **skill** includes an indication of degree of proficiency, either relative or absolute, then **skill** is a quantitative entity. If, on the other hand, no degree of proficiency is included, then **skill** is merely a qualitative entity; that is, its only purpose is to establish the existence of proficiency. The sketch is interpreted as follows:

- Any **employee** may possess any number of skills.
- Any one **machine** may be related to any number of persons who are skilled in its use.
- A specific skill can, and must, be related to one and only one employee and to one and only one machine.
- The arrow joining the **employee** and **skill** represents, collectively, all of the individual sets of **skills** possessed by each **employee.**
- The arrow joining **machine** and **skill** represents, collectively, all of the individual sets of **skills** "owned" by each **machine.**

The arrow represents a set class, that is, a collection of individual sets which are logically identical, in that they relate the same kind of entities in precisely the same way. In the sketch, these set classes are named to indicate their meaning, namely **skill list** and **operator list.** The **skill** is classified by **employee** and **machine.** Figure 3-2 is an expansion of the sketch in terms of a matrix or table. The elements (entries) are the equivalent of the **skill** entity. Each row is

Employees \ Machines	Drill press	Fork lift	Hydraulic press	Turret lathe	Enamel oven
John Smith	×		×	×	
Harry Jones		×			
Gerry Davis	×	×			×
H.R. Prentis	×		×	×	×
Do Little					
H. Harris	×	×	×	×	×

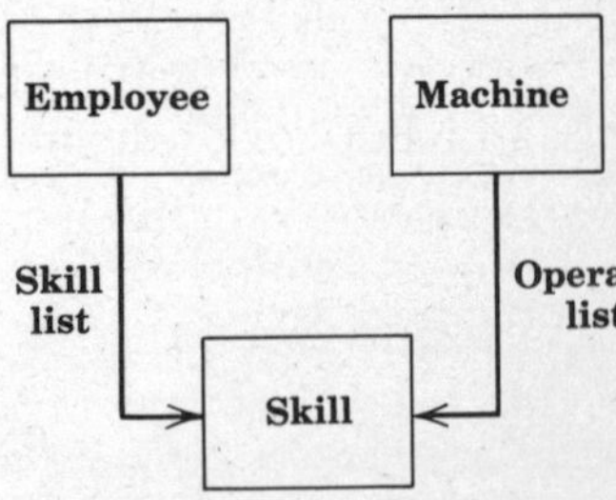

Figure 3-2 **Example of employee/skill/machine relationship.**

equivalent to a single **employee** entity; a column, a **machine.** Each of the nonblank entries in a given row is equivalent to the members of the **skill list** set for a specific **employee;** all of the rows considered as a group are equivalent to the **skill list** set class of the previous sketch. Similar equivalence exists for a specific column and all columns as a collection. The **operator list** (a single column) is the set for a specific machine and a **set class** (all columns) for **machines** in general.

Note that the physical orientation, the size of the boxes, and the shape and/or length of the arrows is unimportant. The designer is free to use or abuse his artistic inclinations as he chooses. The names placed on arrows and in boxes are significant only as a means of improving the communication of the meaning and use of the entity and set classes.

The final group of basic forms is used to establish a relationship between entities which are otherwise alike; that is, they are the same type or of the same set. This type of relationship exists as a tree, ring, or network. An example of a tree is a pure hierarchical structure in which any one element may have either zero or one "owner," and may, in turn, "own" any number of the same kind of elements.

The ring structure discussed is that of a logical ring and not a physical implementation for a list processor. Similarly, the following paragraphs which dwell extensively upon relationships between entities of the same class are not meant to imply that trees, rings, and networks do not or cannot exist between dissimilar entities. On the contrary, the previous example is a network while the first example was a tree (albeit, short). These paragraphs are intended to emphasize the importance, in fact the necessity, to represent relationships between like entities in which the relationship is relative and not absolute as in the previous examples.

To illustrate, an organizational chart is used. Figure 3-3 shows a traditional, four-level, organizational hierarchy. A possible structure is one of four different types of entities, for example, **company, department, division, unit,** as shown in Figure 3-4. While this is impulsively natural, it is obviously in conflict with reality since it specifically implies that only **departments** report to a **company.** In the example, units 0010 and 0020 report directly to the **company,** but to call them **departments** is avoiding the issue, and because of the size and authority implied by the title of department, it is functionally incorrect. Similar inconsistencies exist when a unit is assigned directly to a department; a division, directly to the company, and so on. The rigid hierarchy of Figure 3-4 becomes even more untenable if it becomes necessary to add an additional level. This new level may be anywhere in the hierarchy. For example, if the company is acquired by a conglomerate, a new top level is added. If, on the other hand, a management consultant were to recommend breaking units into subunits, then the new level is added at the bottom. The sole purpose of this discussion is to illustrate that most administrative hierarchies are relative and not absolute.

If you examine the characteristics of an organization, it is apparent that regardless of position, an organization

- Has people assigned to it.
- Performs tasks.
- Generates expense and revenue (even though either one may be zero).
- May "own" subordinate organizations.
- May be subordinate to, at most, one other organization.

The desired structure is that shown in Figure 3-5. In this situation we have introduced a modification to the relationship represented by the arrow, that is, the set class. The dashed arrow represents a conditional

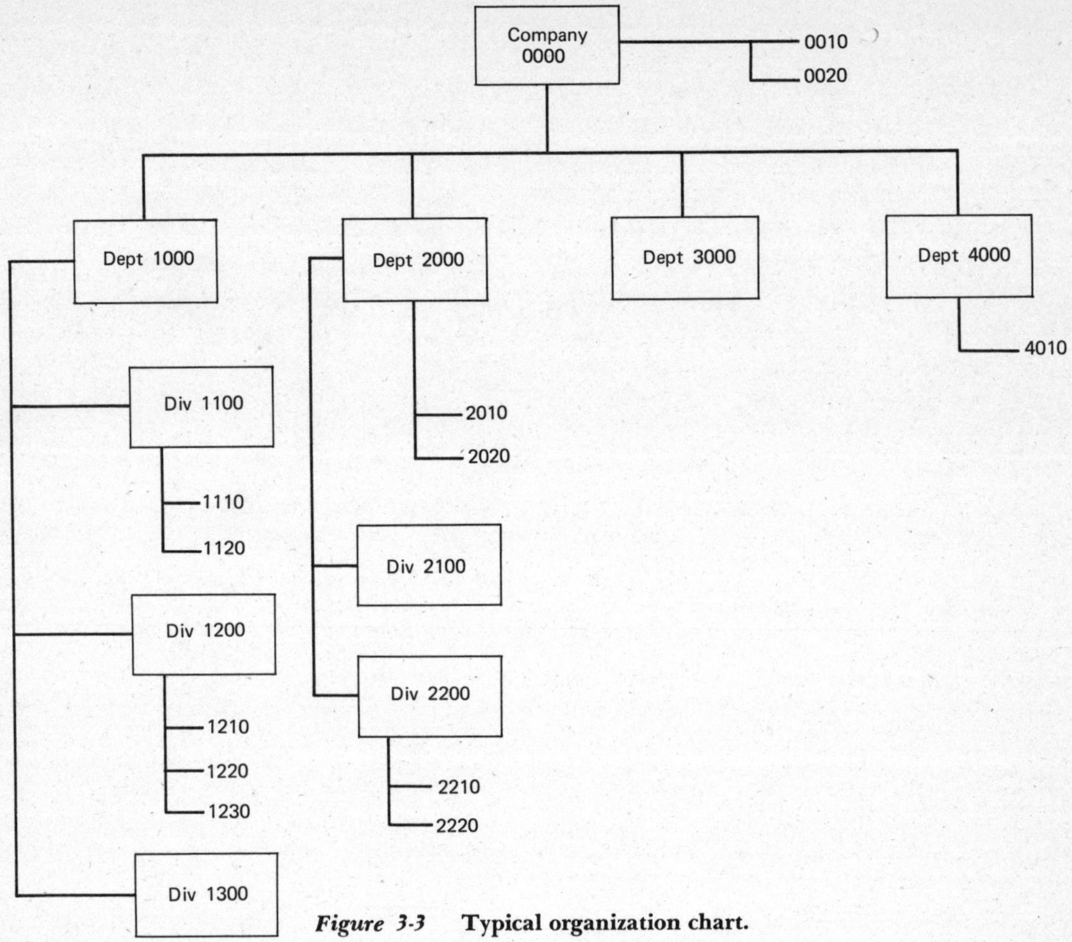

Figure 3-3 **Typical organization chart.**

set. The figure shows that organizations may exist independently of all other organizations. It also indicates that any given organization may be directly subordinate to exactly one other organization and that it may, in turn, "own" any number of subordinate organizations.

If the arrow in Figure 3-5 were solid, rather than dashed, the structure would be that of a ring and not that of a tree. The solid line relationship (see Figure 3-6) is, however, valid if we are describing, for example, a subway route. Note that station A is related to station B in two ways. First, B is "subordinate" to A in that it always follows A. On the other hand, A is subordinate to B in that it comes after B (and C and D and E and F). The route from B to $B1$ is a spur since once taken, it cannot be retraced. It is essential to note that Figure 3-6 establishes dependence and therefore must represent a ring. If any one of the **routes** is nonempty (a route exists from one station to another and is subordinate to some other **station**), then one and only one path exists back to that **station.** The converse is not true, as shown by the spur. This structure does not prohibit a one-station route (e.g., roller coaster or ferris wheel). This structure represents single rings; that is, a station can exist in, at most, one and only one ring. Because an entity in a spur already has an owner, it cannot participate in a ring; it can, however, participate in a tree.

The Network is the last of the structural forms and is similar to the ring and the tree in that it relates two independent entities of the same class. Here, however, any one

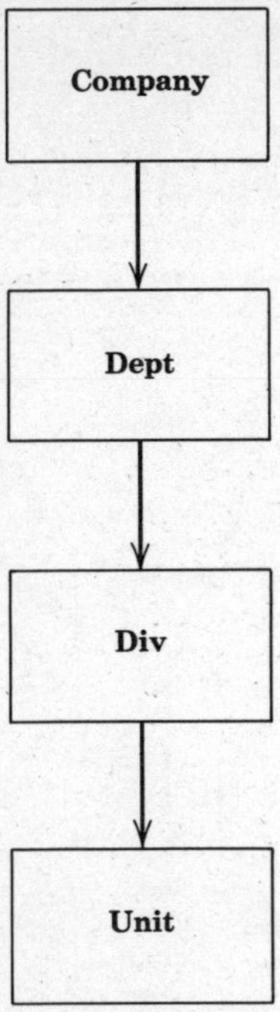

Figure 3-4 **Rigid hierarchy.**

entity may be subordinate to any number of like entities. To illustrate the network we will use as an example an airline. The three different kinds of entities are

- **Airport**
- **Segment**
- **Flight**

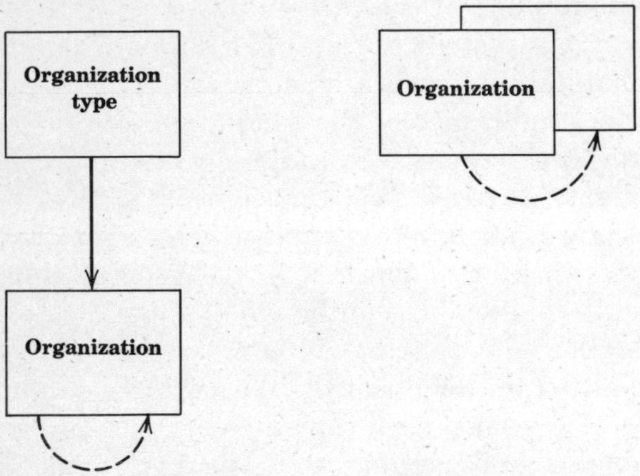

Figure 3-5 **Flexible hierarchy.**

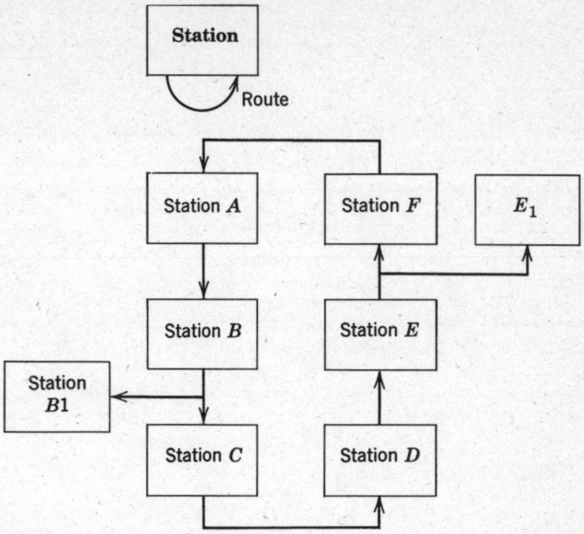

Figure 3-6 **Routing example.**

The structure in Figure 3-7 represents its schedule.

A flight segment or leg is dependent upon the simultaneous existence of two airports (one for take-off and one for landing) and a planned flight. (Note that a training flight can logically have the same origin and destination.) The collection (set) of all segments for any one flight is its route. The collection of all such sets is the set class: **route.** Cities or airports are related by **segments.** However, the relationship is that of a network rather than a tree since the same city can be the origin or destination of flights to any combination of cities. Another view of Figure 3-7 views the **from** set for any **airport** as the departure schedule and the **to** set as the arrival schedule. The general network structure is as follows:

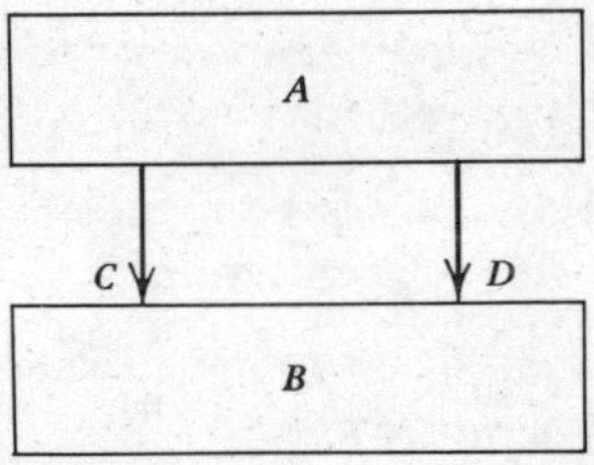

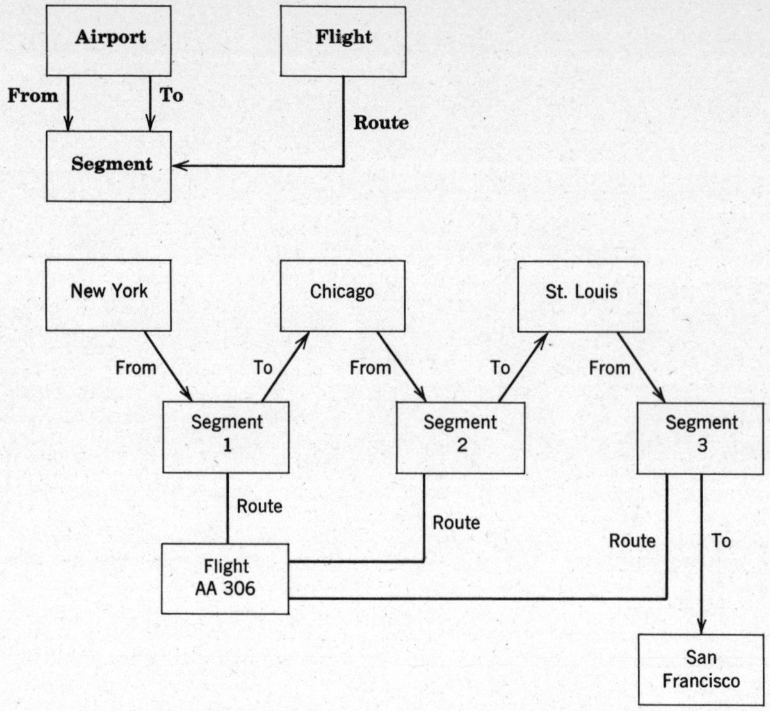

Figure 3-7 **Structure of an airline flight.**

This structure is equally applicable in the following situations:

	A	B	C	D
Accounting	General ledger account	Journal entry	Debit	Credit
Parts list	Material item	Quantity required	Parts list	Where used
Pert/CPM	Event	Activity	Before	After

A full structure diagram is created by combining the basic forms as required by the particular situation. The following are a brief summary of the "rules" of structuring:

- An **entity** may be a member of any number of different **set classes.**
- An **entity** may be an owner of any number of different **set classes.**
- A **set class** may have as members any number of different **entity** classes.
- A **set class** may have alternate **entity classes** as an **owner.**

In this latter case, any specific member of such a set will have only one owner. While the alternate owner situation is conceptually possible, it is the exception rather than the rule. A possible situation is that of a railroad switching yard in which any given freight car can belong to any one of three kinds of owner: **inbound** trains, **outbound** trains, or a **holding** string.

Note that a **freight car** can be subordinate to only one of the three kinds of entities at any one instant in time. The only reason for maintaining such a structure is to preserve the significance of the kind of owner. If the ownership type is not significant in its own right, then the alternative structure of Figure 3-9 is more appropriate. There are three different entities in the **type of train** class—inbound, outbound, and holding string. As a string of cars arrives in the yards (an inbound train), a portion (or all) of the string may remain connected to the engine and become an outbound train. If Figure 3-8 is used to represent the structure,

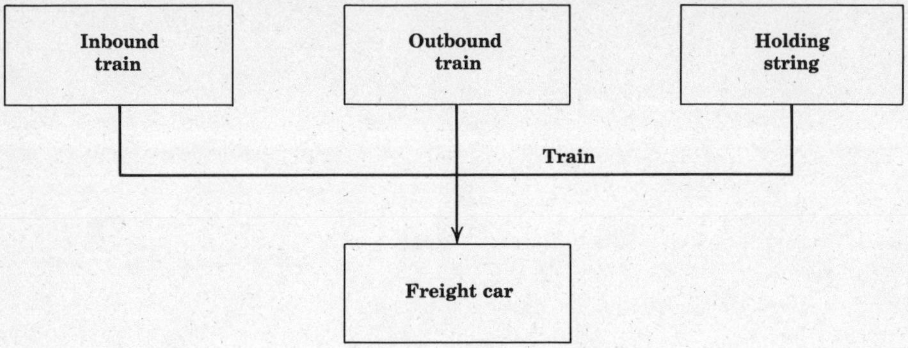

Figure 3-8 **Alternate owner example.**

the string identity is not maintained, and cars must be "switched" individually between classes rather than as a string. If the structure of Figure 3-9 is used, the entire string may be changed by "moving" the train (string) from the Inbound to the Outbound entity.

STRUCTURAL ELEMENTS—AN EXAMPLE

There are only two basic elements in a structure diagram: the **record class** and the **set class.** As an example, consider a paper file in the following situation:

- A four-drawer filing cabinet
- A claims folder, consecutively numbered
- A single claim control sheet containing the claimee's name, and so on, and the name of the insured
- An indeterminate number of claim action sheets—one per action
- A 3 × 5-inch card file which cross indexes the paper file by
  - Coverage type
  - Claimee's name
  - Insured's name
  - Type of accident
  - Hot file

This is a single logical file which is "implemented" by using two different "devices," the four-drawer file and the 3 × 5-inch card file.

The claims control sheet is a record in the four-drawer claims file. It is represented by a single rectangle and labeled **"claim."** The fields within the **claim** record are precisely those of the claims control sheet.

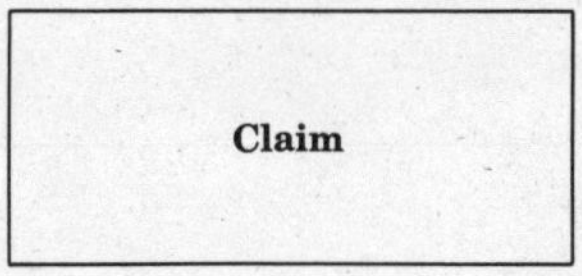

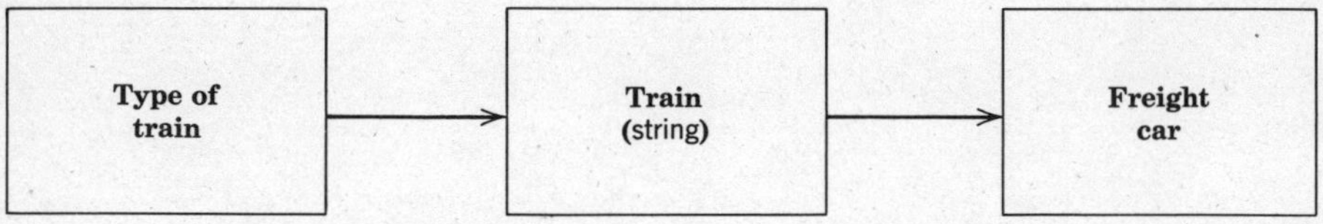

Figure 3-9 **Alternate structure for alternate owner example.**

The second basic type of record in the claim file is the claim action sheet. There can be any number of these for each individual claim, that is, zero, one, two. Logically, it is inconsistent to permit a claim action sheet to exist unless a claim exists (no folder, no place to file the action). A formal relationship obviously exists between these two classes of records, namely, one of ownership and dependence. This relationship is shown by an arrow joining the two rectangles which represent the two record classes.

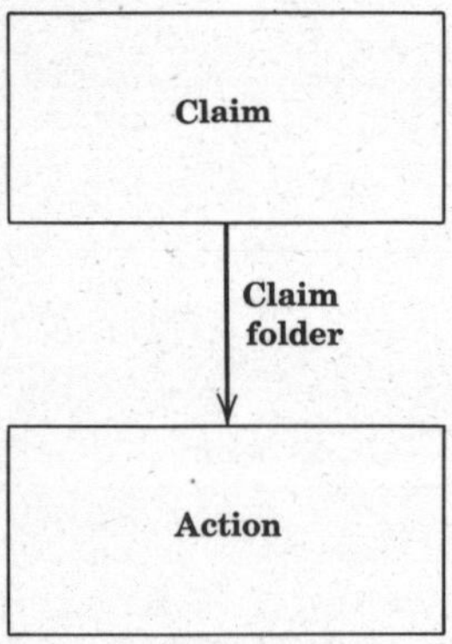

In this case, the relationship is arbitrarily given the name **claim folder**. The naming is arbitrary since the relationship is established by the arrow and not the name.

The direction of the arrow is important because it conveys several strong logical definitions of the relationship:

- Any given **claim** may "own" any number (0, 1, 2, . . . *n*) different **actions**.
- A specific **action** may apply to one and only one **claim**.
- An **action** must have a **claim** as an owner in order to exist.
- The establishment of a **claim** establishes automatically an "empty" **claim folder**. There are no **actions** in it yet.
- If any given **claim** is removed (destroyed) from the file, all of its **actions** are simultaneously removed (analogous to manually removing the folder).
- For each individual **claim** record, its own **set** of **action** records known as the **claim folder** exists.
- Collectively, the **claim** records as a class possess the property of ownership of individual sets of **action** records; that is, it is a **set class**.

If the graphical structure diagram were not used to represent the claims file, it would be necessary to use a less general technique or, even worse, nothing. One such technique is the file layout which would show two different record types—the claim and action records—with a set of common fields which are used as sort key, such as that shown in Figure 3-10. While it may be argued, with some righteousness, that the file layout is sufficient, it does not forcefully convey the necessary concept of ownership and dependence.

A second method, which is less general than the structure diagram but which still

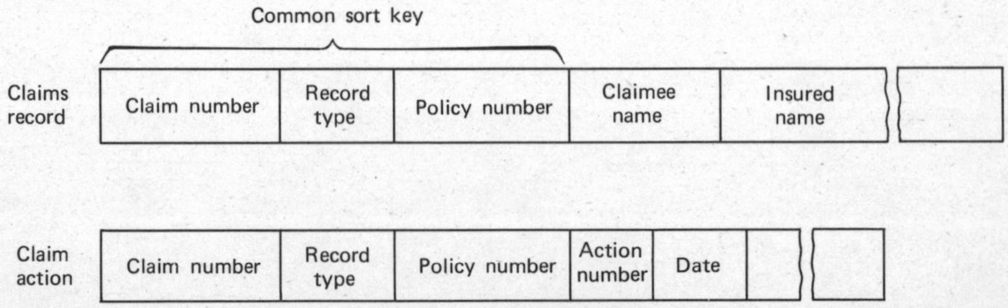

Figure 3-10 **File layout.**

retains the ownership/dependence relationships, is shown in Figure 3-10. Note that the figure clearly conveys the ownership/dependence relationship, the existence of many **claim** records, each with its own set of **actions**, and an indefinite number of **actions** for each **claim**. While either of these two pictorial representations may be satisfactory in any given, though simple, situation, their use becomes either difficult or worthless as the file becomes more complex. As a matter of fact, this is a convenient point to complicate the file by adding a representation of the physical file and each of the file drawers. The file drawer acts as a file divider which facilitates access to the contents of the file. If dividers are placed within the drawer, even more rapid access to any given claim will be achieved. This new class of records is designated as a **divider**.

The two classes of records to the left of the dotted line were incorporated to represent, logical, indexing which solely exists to facilitate access. If a file layout were drawn for this situation, it would be identical to Figure 3-10 simply because there is no way to recognize within the file the existence of the file divider. If the diagramming of Figure 3-11 were used the concepts of ownership and indexing for access would be conveyed, but as the number of types of records increase, the number of sketches rises exponentially. For those with a physical bent, note that the addition of the two record types represents a form of two-level indexed sequential. Specifically, given a claim number, find the correct cabinet; having found the cabinet, find the correct divider within the cabinet; and having found the correct divider, find the correct claim within the correct divider, within the correct cabinet.

Figure 3-13 is an example of logical indexing rather than the physical sequential indexing of Figure 3-12. Both are used to speed the process of accessing any given record—the sequential indexing when the identifier (claim number) is known; the logical indexing, when the properties are known. Because logical indexing, used to determine identity, is the inverse of the sequential indexing, used to determine properties, the structure in Figure 3-13 is called

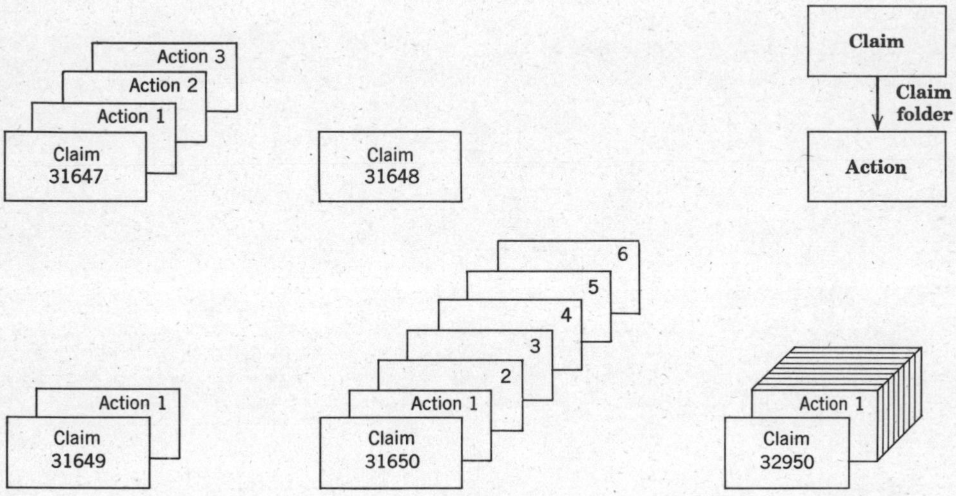

Figure 3-11

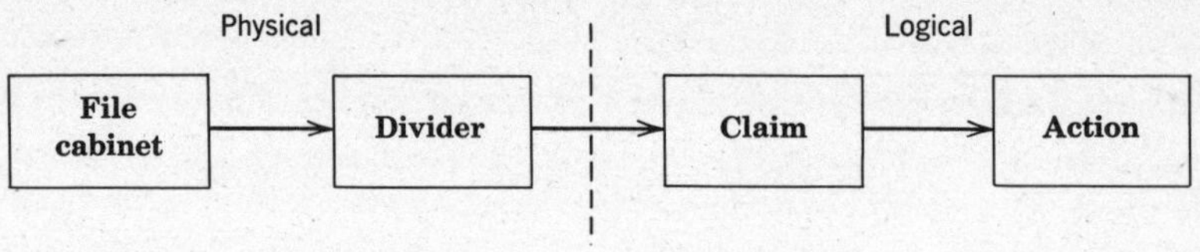

Figure 3-12 **Use of indexing.**

an inverted file. Specifically, the file of Figure 3-12 is inverted on the five attributes:

- Insured
- Claimant
- Coverage
- Accident
- "Hot" type

Figure 3-13 implies that for any given **claim** record in the paper file, as many as five **claim*** records may exist in the card file. Unfortunately, there is no warranty that each claim will exist, that is, be categorized or cross indexed for each category. As shown, the card file contains 10 different record types, five of which (the indices) are "owned" directly by the "file"; that is, they have a common owner.

As long as the claim number is known, it is possible to locate the desired folder; however, if an inquiry is made of the file for which the claim number is unknown, search becomes cumbersome. For example, a question is raised concerning the number and details of claims filed by one person; that is, is there evidence of insurance fraud? With the file sequenced on claim number it is necessary to examine each **claim** record in turn to determine the name of the claimant. Note that it is necessary to examine every record in spite of the sequential indexing.

In order to facilitate query, the 3×5-inch card file, or, at least, its logical equivalent is employed. Specifically, the cards are used to **cross index** the file. In this case, the file will be indexed on

- Type of coverage
- Claimant's name
- Insured's name
- Accident type
- HOT file

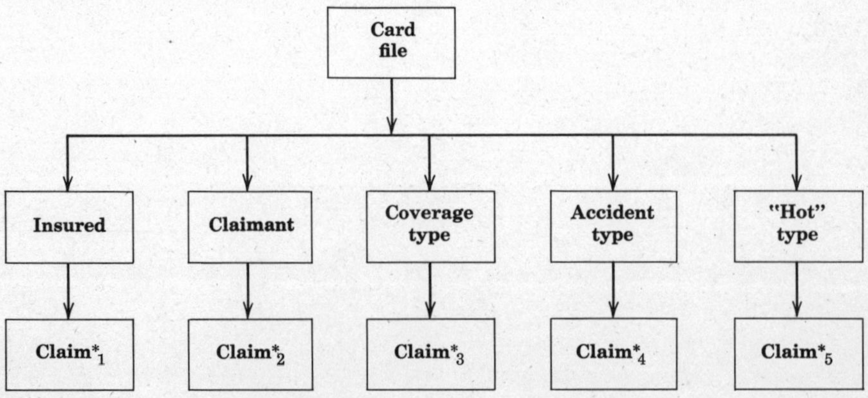

Figure 3-13 **Cross index of card file.**

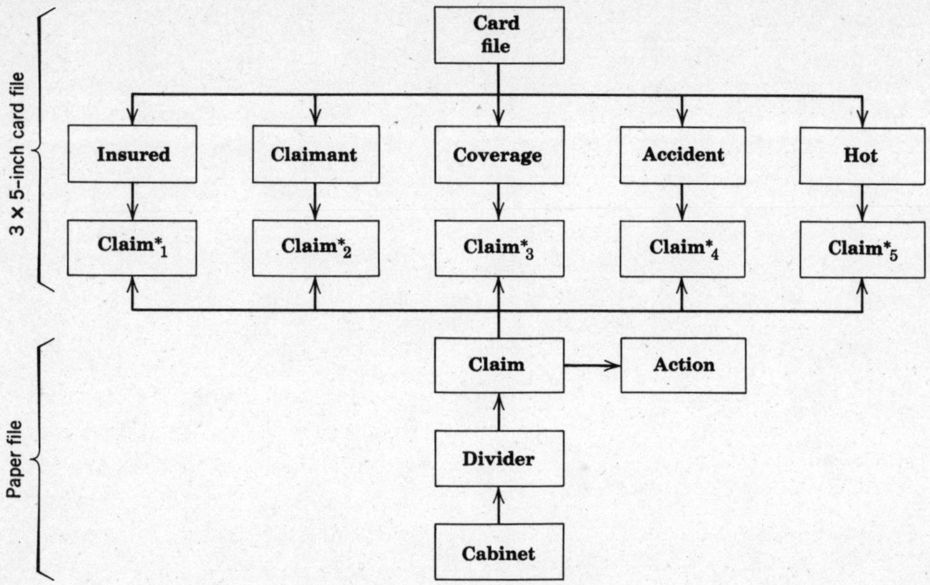

Figure 3-14 **Integrated file structure.**

As seen by now, each of these five types of indexing represents a record class and the relationship between the **claim** and the indices will represent five separate **relationship** classes. Using the graphical notation we have the integration into one data base, the sequential file and the inverted file of Figure 3-13. This is shown in Figure 3-14.

STRUCTURE AND IMPLEMENTATION

It should be obvious that a structure diagram has little more than academic value unless there is at least an informal correlation between the logical and physical structure. The previous section implied such an implementation with the four-drawer and 3×5-inch card files.

As implied in the previous sections, each **entity class** is normally implemented as a separate type of record; each with its own length, identifiers, and fields. The set (arrow) is implemented either by explicit indexing (an address or an access key) or implicitly by position, relative to the owner. When a record is a dependent member in more than one set class, it is necessary either to repeat the record for each such set or to identify one set as the "primary" and then use some form of indexing for the other sets. The primary set is indicated with a double lined arrow (as below, see **the route**).

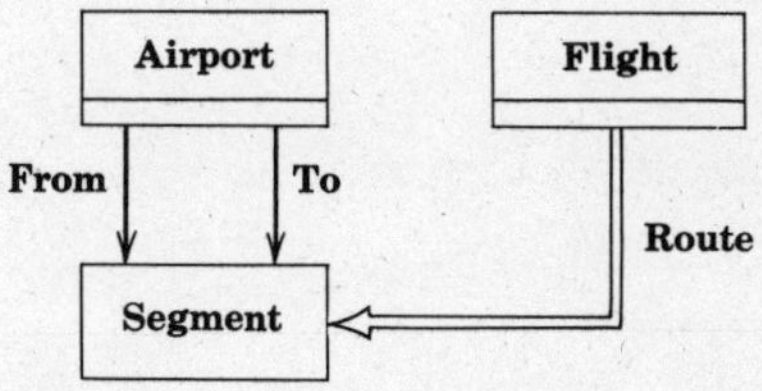

The double line in the entity (record) box is used to indicate that the record is directly accessible and that the identifier (access key) is unique for that entity class. This kind of record may be accessed by

- Computing an address from the access key
- Looking up its address in a table
- "Remembering" its address

Such records are normally referred to as file entry points. One such technique for accessing records is known as indexed sequential. While this technique is discussed later, its logical structure for two and four levels of indexing follows.

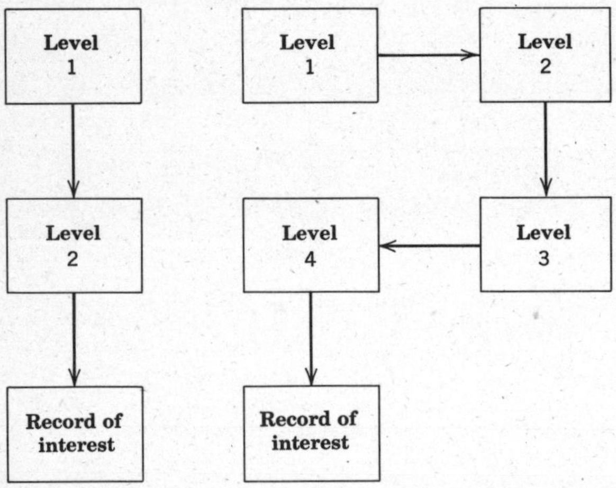

Each level is analogous to a table whose entries contain a range of values and the "address" of the next lower level.

The structure can also be implemented using a list in which each of the owner records acts as the head of a list of the member records. As implied in the previous paragraphs, each **flight** record is the head of a list of **segment** records. Each **airport** record leads two lists, **from** and **to,** but these lists may consist either of redundant copies of the full **segment** record or of an abbreviated record containing only a reference to the appropriate **segment** record.

If the airline structure is implemented such that each **flight** record headed a list of **segment** records which contain, in addition to the normal segment data, the address or access key to the next record in each of the three lists (**route, to, from**) in which it is a member, then the structure is known as knotted or threaded list.

Regardless of the technique used to implement the structure, it is important for a direct and obvious correlation to exist between the logical structure and the eventual physical organization. If a purely sequential implementation is used, each box represents a separate type of record, and the arrow, a header-trailer relationship. If a record-type is dependent upon two or more other types, it is necessary to provide redundantly the data of all but one of its owners in each such dependent record or to maintain separate master files for each such owner with the dependent record duplicated in each. Non-sequential implementations are possible via the various manufacturers and software houses packages such as Honeywell-G.E.'s Integrated Data Store, IBM's IMS, Burrough's FORTE, and so on. Typical of such languages is the CODASYL Data Base Task Group's language.

SECTION 4

Modeling– The Basis for Design

The system designer must understand the relationships among the elements of an application in order to create a viable design. This section introduces the concept of a "model" as an aid to understanding the elements of a data base and their interrelationships. A project control system (C/S PCS) is the basis for a model employing the notational conventions of Section 3. The role of the model is emphasized as a means of crystalizing the application for the user and designer alike, and, more importantly, as a means of ensuring that any resulting data base is feasible and will survive. Too many applications are data and/or management-dependent; a change in either will cause the untimely demise of a data base and all of its supporting and dependent software.

In this section, the concept of data independence is introduced. The means of encouraging and achieving data independence are described and illustrated with specific examples. This section also emphasizes (and illustrates) the means of achieving procedural independence of programs and data through structure. While not always apparent, the concept of modeling in data base design is the key to machine and device independence.

THE MODEL—A HEURISTIC DEFINITION

In Section 3, the role of the structure diagram as a method of communicating the characteristics and content of a data base was emphasized. This section is dedicated to the role of the structure diagram as a design tool.

In the example of the claims file, the structure diagram was used to illustrate the relationship between the paper file (four-drawer) and the indexed file (3 × 5-inch cards). However, the final diagram Figure 3-14 was, in fact, the logical representation of the operating environment of that paper system. During the past decade, much of the work in management science has been devoted to the task of describing, evaluating, and optimizing mathematical representations of business or restricted facets of business. The techniques, technology, and art of describing a business are collectively known as modeling. This is precisely the process which is used in creating the file structure diagram. Since the file structure diagram describes the relationships between entities, for example, people and claims, it is, in fact, a model.

At this point, it is certainly appropriate to accept the file structure diagram as a model, but at the same time to ask, "a model of what?" In the case of the claims system, it was, perhaps, a model of the environment within which that information system was to exist. If, however, that manual system were to be automated, the file structure diagram would be unchanged (albeit, the titles might change). Then this would imply two important characteristics of the model: first, the model is independent of implementation; second, it is a logical representation of the whole business (or some segment). The term, business, is obviously much too restrictive to apply to the model; it should be environment. Since the structure diagram is logical, not physical, then it must represent a qualitative model. The physical file represents the quantitative model. The file diagram and the file itself limit the scope of the environment. This limitation occurs by omission of those entities which the designer considers irrelevant. In the claims example, the environment was limited to claims processing; it did not include or attempt to accommodate the insurance company as a whole. The file structure diagram is a definitive representation of the environment.

COST/SCHEDULE PLANNING AND CONTROL—AN EXAMPLE

The problems associated with the conduct of development projects have both plagued and intrigued management. The magnitude of these problems, in terms of dollars and time, led to the creation of a variety of techniques which attempted to aid management in measuring the progress of development projects. In many cases, these management techniques were, themselves, development projects sponsored primarily by the Department of Defense during and following World War II. In many cases, these techniques considered time and cost as separate measures of progress. The success or failure of a developmental project is, however, determined by both the time and the cost required to achieve a specific goal.

The Cost/Schedule Planning and Control System (C/S PCS) is one of the more recent attempts to

- Rapidly identify potentially undesirable cost or time overruns
- Measure more accurately the "value of work performed"; that is, progress
- Document planned cost and schedules at the level of measurement
- Document the time and cost impact of changes to the plan

Since a C/S PCS requires both cost and time information, it is necessary to combine the accountant's traditional dollar measures and the time measures of the project engineer.

In order to illustrate the design a C/S

PCS, a model of a project environment, will be developed and tested. The testing will be logical and will ensure that the model is accurate and sufficient. In our example the project environment will be described in terms of contracts; that is, it assumes development of equipment or techniques which is sponsored by the Department of Defense (or some similar governmental agency) as the result of competitive bidding. It is further assumed that the contract was awarded on the basis of a proposal which specified not only a time schedule of achievement but also the cost for each step.

If the basic premise of C/S PCS is examined closely, it should be possible to identify the critical information element. Both the time and cost schedule of a development project must be expressed in terms of a measurable event. For C/S PCS, this measurable event is known as a Work Element or Task. The depth of detail to which the Development Effort is described in terms of tasks will depend upon the magnitude of the contract, the contrariness of the customer, and the uncertainty (technical risk) of the project. The level at which the project is scheduled should, however, be consistent with the level at which progress can be measured; that is, cost and time. After all, the purpose of planning is to permit management to control, rather than to generate, the world's largest event chart.

The task is the basic element of a C/S PCS. Tasks are related to each other in a hierarchy, which is commonly called a Work Breakdown Structure (WBS). From a purely logical point of view, a task can always be considered a collection of other tasks until, finally, the entire contract is called a task.

A task, which can be a scheduled element or a collection of such elements, may be associated with organizations in two ways: responsibility and performance. Good management principles demand that each task "belong" to only one organization; this is responsibility. At the same time, one or more other organizations can be scheduled to do the work—performance. For example, Engineering is responsible for building a new engine, but the machine shop fabricates the rotors and so on.

Figure 4-1 is the model of our environment to the extent to which it has been defined. Starting with the **task**, we note the following:

- It is uniquely identified (double underlined box).
- It must belong to one, and only one, contract to exist (work statement).
- It must also belong to only one organization in order to exist (responsibility).
- It may be related to other tasks in a tree structure (**work breakdown**—dotted arrow).
- It may be related to one or more organizations ("?" arrow, "?" entity, and **perform**) for actual performance.

Before proceeding with the rest of the struc-

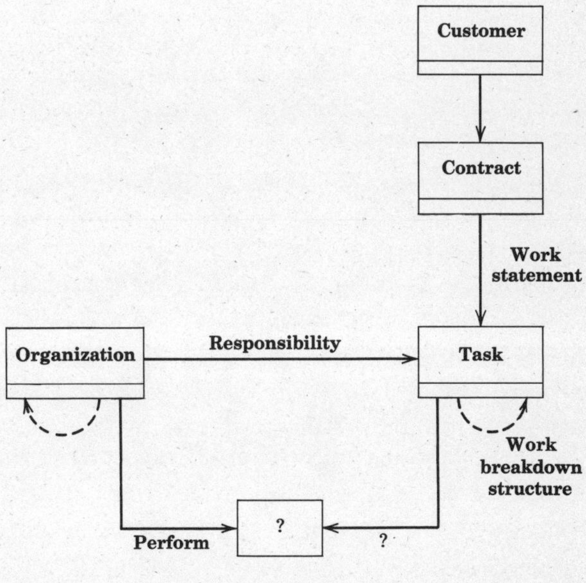

Figure 4-1 **Preliminary model of C/S PCS environment.**

ture, there are several alternative structures that should be examined. First, a **task** is directly associated with the **organization**, as follows:

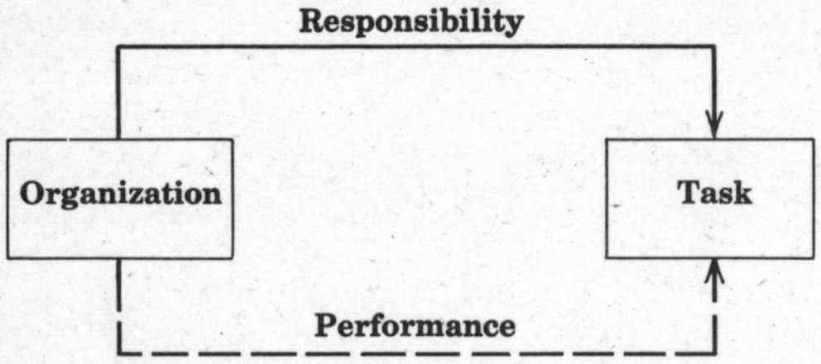

While the dashed line for the **performance** relationship states that a **task** can be defined, even though it has not been assigned to any one organization for implementation, it unduly restricts the capability to assign the same task to more than one organization for implementation.

A second alternative would reverse the roles of the **organization** and **task:**

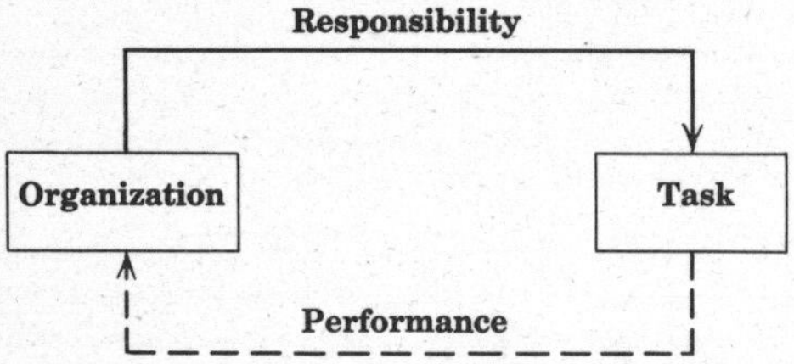

This would restrict any one organization to work on, at most, only one task. It should be obvious that neither of these alternatives is correct or acceptable.

An accurate model of the interaction of organizations and tasks must permit any organization to perform work on any number of tasks, and simultaneously, to permit any one task to be associated with any number of organizations. Thus some form of logical relationship (the box with the question mark) does actually exist. In terms of a schedule or an event-oriented network, this relationship is known as a milestone, that is, the dated occurrence of a significant event. The relationship between a task and its events is a schedule.

The tree structure indicated in Figure 4-1 by the dashed arrow, **work breakdown structure,** states that the schedule for any task includes automatically the schedule for all of its subordinate tasks. This aspect of a tree structure is frequently neglected in many information systems in the name of efficiency. The tendency is to summarize upward in a hierarchy. Such summarization is not only wasteful in terms of memory (file space) and logically questionable, but also guarantees data inconsistency. This inconsistency arises when someone, usually the boss, discovers that the report showing the details does not add up to the value given in another report based on the summary. Such inconsistency is usually explained (albeit unsuccessfully to the boss) in terms of the maintenance program or in terms of time phasing of summary and detail data maintenance. There are times when an implementation decision is made to carry summary data, but not in this section which is directed solely to the logical design. Similar comments apply to the organizational hierarchy.

Regarding hierarchies, there is a tendency to describe both the organizational and work breakdown structures as fixed, rather than relative hierarchies. This tendency is usually founded on the rather narrow outlook which comes from creating clever coding schemes which incorporate intelligence into identification numbers. It is conceded that such coding is desirable for sorting purposes, but it should not be an impediment to the thought process.

In one actual implementation, the structure of the C/S PCS data base was modeled after the coding scheme used in the firm's accounting system. This structure (Figure 4-2) reflects the rigid hierarchy imposed by the account structure. Needless to say, the system was hardly loaded when the number of exceptions to the fixed tree structure exceeded the number of instances where it fit. There is nothing wrong with taking advan-

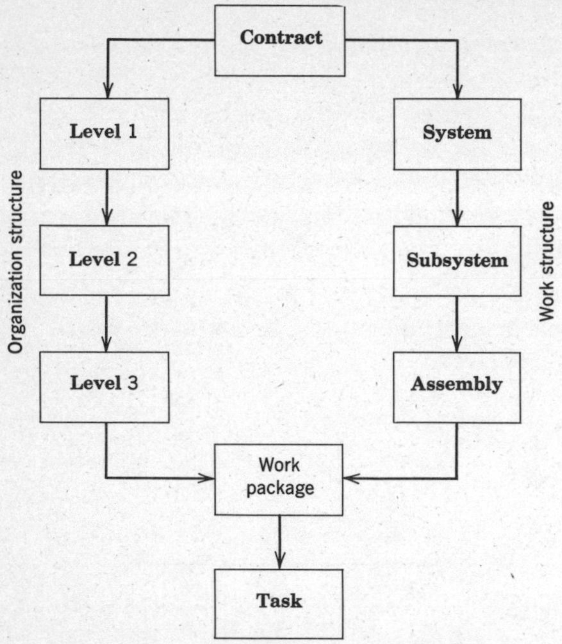

Figure 4-2 **Example of fixed hierarchy.**

tage of an existing numbering scheme. The danger arises when such a numbering scheme forces a solution which does not exactly fit the problem. If the numbering scheme is to be employed, it should be part of the solution and not part of the problem.

A closer inspection of the structure of Figure 4-2 will show several logical traps. Specifically, the following:

- Only level 3 organizations may perform work.
- The organization structure as a whole can work on only one contract (the common owner).
- No overhead or management organizations can exist unless there is a contract.
- No one has responsibility for the contract, system, subsystem, or assembly.
- The system cannot tolerate graceful expansion in level of detail.
- Work (tasks) cannot be planned in advance of assignment.

In general, fixed hierarchial structures exist only in the mind of the planner. They are very rare in practice. The point is simple—do not design yourself into a box.

The structure of Figure 4-1 can now be expanded by adding the provision for monetary data as the following:

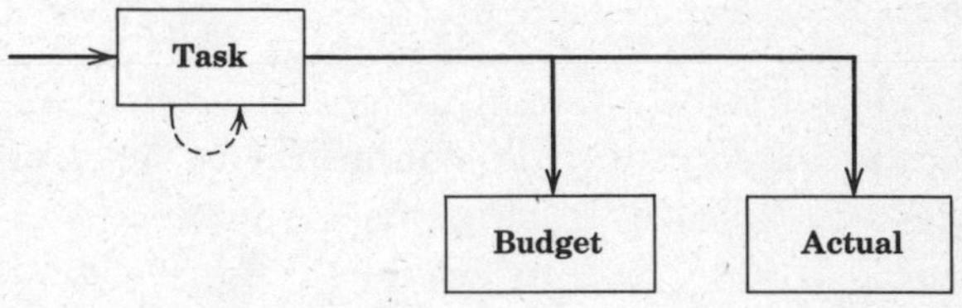

Two different entity classes have been shown reflecting the existence of two different kinds of money. Any one task can "own" any number of such entities; for example, one budget for each month of the task. Likewise, any given task can possess both budget and actual costs.

The structure of Figure 4-1 establishes the relationships which actually exist in a project environment; namely,

- An organization may be assigned responsibility for any number of tasks.
- An organization may actually work on any number of tasks, which may be the same as those assigned for responsibility.
- An organization implicitly performs and/or is responsible for all the tasks of its subordinate organizations.
- An organization, regardless of its relative position within the hierarchy, is logically as capable of performing or exercising responsibility as any other organization.
- The "list" of milestones which are associated with any one organization represents its schedule of work.
- The "list" of milestones which are associated with any one task represents its implementation schedule.
- Any one task must be assigned to one and only one organization for responsibility and through milestones to any number for performance.

- The schedule for any task includes the sum of the schedules of all its subordinate tasks.

EXTENSIONS TO THE BASIC MODEL

The basic model of Figure 4-1 is extended easily to include a full event network, cost accounting, configuration control, and marketing intelligence. An event network is intended to establish the order in which tasks must occur and the planned duration of each activity. If we recast the connection between **tasks** and **organizations** as an **activity,** then an **activity** can be viewed as a sequence of events. Events within the same activity and from other activities are related to each other in the sense that there is a restrictive order in which they can occur. In the simplest case the event "start" must always precede the event "stop" for the same activity. Likewise, the activity "excavate" must precede the activity "pour foundation." It is quite common that more than one event from many activities follows any given activity. This network of events is the basis for scheduling work and for evaluating the impact of work slippage.

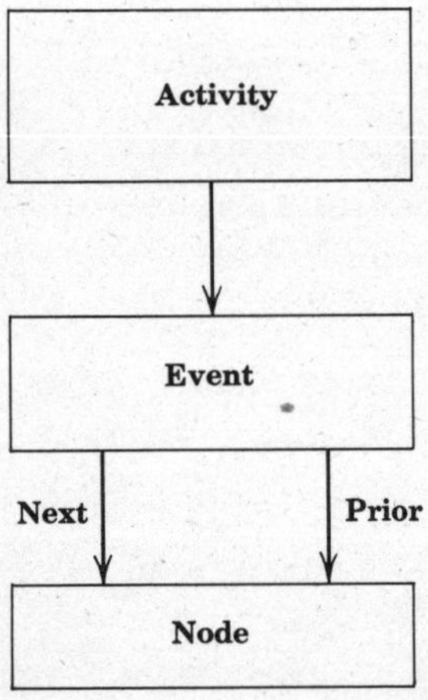

The duration of an activity is the difference between the time of its first and last event. The **next** and **prior** association of an **event** and **node** is nothing more than a precedence matrix which establishes the required order. Note that it is possible for many events to have the same prior event and vice versa.

Coordinated cost accounting is accomplished by relating (or classifying) the actual cost of a task to the appropriate general ledger account (or subledger) as follows:

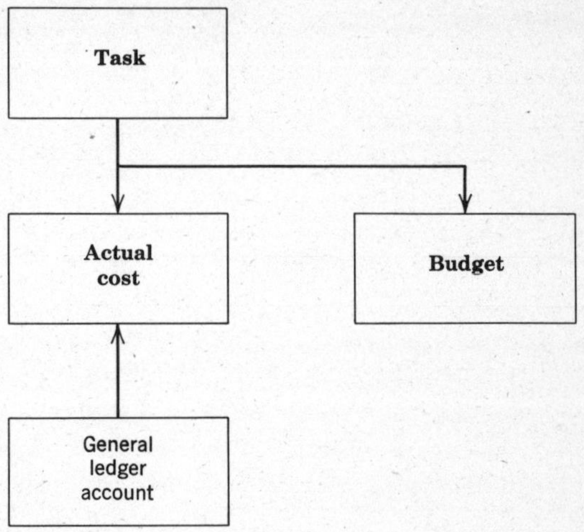

Configuration control is concerned with maintaining the identity of equipment and the modifications/variations. This is accomplished by establishing a relationship between a task and a piece of equipment as follows:

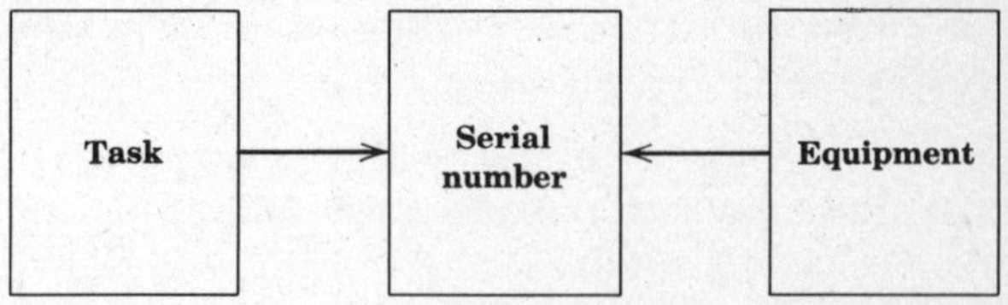

Finally, a degree of market intelligence is established by relating all customers with the equipment and by viewing equipment or products as a hierarchy, that is, a product line. The final structure is shown in Figure 4-3.

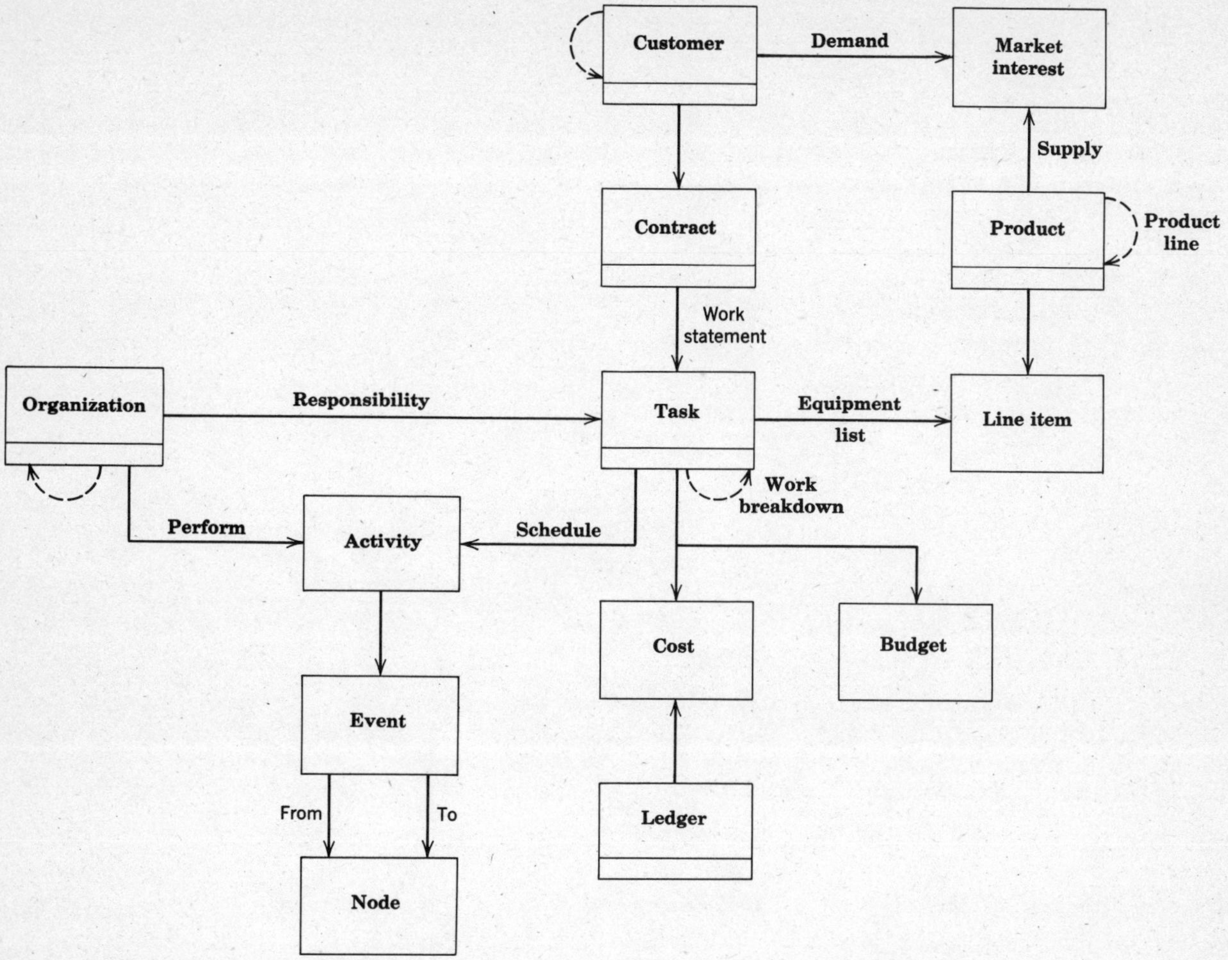

Figure 4-3 **Intermediate C/S PCS environment.**

DATA INDEPENDENCE

The logical structure (model) of the C/S PCS environment is independent of the physical data which may, at some time, be present within any implementation. Observe that at no time during the discussion was any reference made to, or reliance placed on, either the amount of data or the actual values expected. If the structure diagram is a model of the environment, it must be independent of the size of the project or the number of projects. At the same time, it must not presuppose any intelligence in the way identifiers of tasks or organizations are assigned. (Note that the structure does not preclude such intelligence).

SECTION 5

Physical Organization–The Basis of Implementation

Each of the preceding sections has dealt with the important problems of defining the elements of the data base and their interrelationships. These sections have attempted to link the design to reality in order to produce a viable and survivable data base. The design sketches have been completed; now the specifications must be prepared.

This section serves as the transition between the logical structure and the world of hardware limitations. The salient characteristics of mass storage devices are outlined with particular emphasis on their relationships to the problems of data base design.

This section is the introduction to the practical implementation techniques of physical organization for managing physical space through indices and tables, compression and rearrangement, and for the equally important management of the data records, that is, storage retrieval, update and deletion through list, indices, tables, and chaining.

This section will also highlight the effects of file design on data independence; data redundancy, preallocation of physical space, transferability, recovery and restart, logical and/or physical reorganization, recovery/restart, and multiple access.

MASS STORAGE AND THE FACTS OF LIFE

In Section 2 the concept of an information space was introduced. As mentioned, information is conveniently described in terms of the three dimensions: **entity**, **attribute**, and **value**. Unfortunately, memory devices tend to be one-dimensional.

But even if they were multidimensional, the density of information elements, in all but the most contrived of cases, is low enough so that a multidimensional device would have such a low utilization that either cost or lack of speed would make prohibitive its use.

Mass storage devices in use today, with the exception of bulk core, are based on physical motion of magnetic materials. In fact, it is the presence of motion that places an inherent, practical limit on the speed of such devices. This mechanical motion is either linear (start and stop), as in the case of tape, or rotational as with a disk or drum. There are generally two numbers which are important when discussing the "speed" of a memory device; namely, average access time and transfer rate. The latter refers to how fast data can be transferred (read or written) once it has been found. The transfer rate depends in part on the speed of the magnetic material (inches per second), the density of recording (bits or characters per inch), and the number of tracks (e.g., 7 or 9 for tape). The transfer rate of disk, drum, and in some cases even tape approaches the speed of core memories.

The hooker with mass storage is its relatively long access time. Access time is normally understood to mean the average time to access a randomly selected piece of data. For a rotating device, this is one half the amount of time it takes to complete one rotation. For example, the access time for a 3600 rpm drum is $8\frac{1}{3}$ msec. Any rotating device must include in addition to rotational delay the average amount of time required to mechanically adjust (move) the reading heads from one "track" to another.

As you recall, the logical design of the data base was conducted with absolutely no consideration of the physical problems of implementation. It is, in fact, conducted as if we had an infinitely large memory which could contain simultaneously all the data required by the system. For the most practical systems, such a luxury will never exist.

The programmer does have, however, two limited resources at his disposal: time and space. Within certain limitations, he can always substitute time for space and vice versa. Such substitution will, however, always result in some losses; that is, a premium or penalty is paid whenever a space/time trade-off is exercised.

The space/time trade-off is made each time a new record type is implemented. In the simplest case, the decision to create an employee record as a header and a series of dependent records as trailers is a space/time trade-off. Namely, an employee record, which is large enough to accommodate the employee with the largest number of dependents, does waste space for all the other employees. Conversely, the use of trailer records for each dependent requires additional processing time and, in addition, requires the use of space for overhead (namely the employee's identifier). As shown in the earlier sections, however, the use of multiple record types (one for each employee and each of his dependents) is correct logically. In this case, it is probably relatively close to being correct physically.

The space/time trade-off becomes even more significant whenever the logical structure indicates that an entity class is associated (i.e., tied by the arrow) with at least two other entity classes. Physically, we are indicating that it is desirable to maintain simultaneously the same information in more than one collation sequence. As soon as that happens, something is sacrificed, either time or space. A second, and perhaps less obvious, situation exists whenever a given entity class is desired to serve as a file-entry point and, at the same time, to relate (the arrow again) to other entities. All entry-point entities are implicitly related to each other.

A problem which is, in reality, related to

the space/time trade-off concerns the problem of "addressing" records within a data base. In a purely sequential file, such as those found on a magnetic tape, addressing is always done in terms of direction, that is, next or prior. The only addressing possible is to look at the key and to decide which way to go—forward or backwards. It is seldom possible to determine, by comparing values, how far to go. However, in such a file, there is no empty or unused space reserved for future additions or caused by deletion of existing records.

A random access device is nothing more than a collection of several small sequential devices. Each track on a disk or drum or a word in a core memory is the logical equivalent of a small sequential file. The distinction between random and sequential is really relative, with the former implying the ability to access any segment without regard to the location of the previous access. If a file is placed on such a random access device, then it is possible for the user to construct an addressing scheme for accessing records. For example, most of today's time-sharing systems gives the user the ability to create and access random files. In this context, a random file is a contiguous segment of mass storage (it contains all possible physical addresses between and including its starting and ending addresses). In such cases the user defines a fixed record size and the maximum number of records to be placed in the file; the system will then compute the total required space, allocate, and create the file. In this case, a file is created by equating the file name to a starting address and carrying the size and maximum number of records as an attribute. The user only needs to identify the number (e.g., the 346th) of the record, and the system can determine which one he wants, whether or not it exists, and then access it. While such a technique of relative addressing may seem neat and tidy to the user, it does leave a few loose ends in the area of space management and restricts unnecessarily the file to a single record size.

A second attempt at addressing, relies on the use of indices or access keys. An access key is nothing more than one or more named data fields which permit access to a record based on their value(s). The sort key for a sorted sequential (e.g., tape) file is an access key. If more than one record in the file has the same value for an access key, the system permits the user to find the first, based on a "less than/greater than" test.

Indexed access is the use of a table containing an address and the upper and lower values for the access key of a group of records. If, in addition, the access key is a sort key, then the technique is commonly known as indexed sequential. Note that indexed sequential is a physical, not a logical, structure.

A file which is indexed sequential normally requires a minimum of one access to the mass storage device for each level of indexing in order to complete a random search. Indexed sequential is a practical method of achieving relatively fast random access while maintaining simultaneously the intelligence which may exist in the value of an access key. Such intelligence usually exists in such things as part numbers, account numbers, serial numbers, and so on.

A third addressing technique, also using an access key, is known as randomization. To be more precise, it is really a process of calculation which uses the value of the access key to compute an address. The term randomization is applied to such a computation, because if care is used in designing the computation, the addresses which result from the computation process will be randomly distributed across the range of permissible addresses. Ideally, a calculated access key will require one and only one access to the mass storage device in order to find any randomly selected record.

Note the basic distinction between the

results of using a calculated access key and an indexed sequential access key: the randomized access normally requires only one access to find the record while the indexed sequential method requires one for each level of indexing. However, if any subsequent sequential processing is desired, the advantage of randomization is quickly lost; for example, it is desired to locate a record for a specific automobile based on its serial number. Having found the record for that car, examine the records for the 10 cars built before and after it on the same assembly line, that is, find 21 specific records. Pure randomization could require 21 separate accesses to mass storage. Indexed sequential, on the other hand, would require, for four levels of indexing (20 at each level for a total of 160,000 cars per file) about five accesses (one for each level plus a second access at the bottom) or an average of .24 accesses per record. The point is simple: **think!**

A final method of addressing records within a file is to remember its address when it was stored. Such a technique is aptly named direct addressing. It should be obvious that the disadvantage of using such a technique is simply the problem of remembering its address.

SPACE MANAGEMENT

The previous discussion on addressing neatly avoided the tacky problems that must be faced whenever a record is stored or deleted, namely, the management of physical space. In the case of the time-sharing system's random file, there is no problem; the user creates a new record and specifies its address, which is either valid and vacant or invalid. And when the user deletes a record from the file, it disappears. That description of file management may well be the manner in which files are considered by a time-sharing system, but if the user accepts such a simplistic view he soon discovers that he has no file. The time-sharing system has not provided a file system, but merely a method of logically addressing mass storage.

The creation of new records and deletion of old ones are basic to two levels of space management, physical and logical. Consider what is required in order to establish a new record in a file. First, the "space manager" must determine where such a record should be placed. In the case of indexed sequential, this involves working down through the indices until the logical position (relative to all other records) is determined. At this point one of two alternatives is available.

- Physically insert the record into its sequential position by physically moving records within that block in order to make room for it.
- Physically insert a "pointer" to the record so that the logical sequence is maintained, and place the record in an overflow area.

Most indexed sequential space management schemes rely heavily upon the use of an initial load which will distribute the records in some "optimum" fashion and, simultaneously, create the indices. Provision may be made within the physical record (block) to accommodate a predetermined number of new records (i.e., space for new records is reserved). As this space is used through the addition of new records, overflow can be assigned to a system expansion area or the full block can be physically split with half the records remaining in the original block and the other half being assigned to a new block. In either case, the optimum load distribution of the file can be expected to deteriorate as records are added and deleted.

The randomized method of accessing records would, in storing a new record, compute an address based on the access key. This is the desired location for a new record. It is possible, however, that some other record has already been stored at that address, thus requiring a method to handle the overflow. Normally, a search for space will be made in ascending address sequence and the new record will be "chained" to the first record which randomized to that address. Chained means that a field in the record is reserved for the address of the overflow record.

In the case of the time-sharing random file, it was the user's responsibility to keep track of available space. This may involve the creation and maintenance of a table which identifies each possible record address and its status. This is obviously undesirable for a large file and becomes more difficult with data bases which consist of many different kinds and sizes of records. In such cases, the space manager does not attempt control at the logical record level but, rather, attacks the problem at the level of physical transfer—the block. It is quite common in many file management systems to maintain a space inventory at the block level and then provide for logical records within the block. Space within a block can then be allocated independently of the rest of the file.

When a file is broken down into physical records (blocks or pages), the housecleaning and bookkeeping tasks associated with the storage of new records and, more importantly, the removal of old records is greatly facilitated.

IMPLEMENTATION OF LOGICAL ASSOCIATIONS

The previous two sections stressed the importance of logical associations. While such concepts are valuable and in some cases an absolute necessity, they can cause nightmares for the implementor. In general, only two techniques are available for implementation: the list and the knotted list. While the distinction is not always discernible, the level of shouting and the heat generated in all but the most sedate discussions of the subject would indicate that the perceived distinction is important, either through experience or ignorance.

The list is a sequence of records. The method used to go from record to record may rely on

- Contiguous placement as in a sorted tape file
- Reference by access key
- Chaining by address

In any event, it is necessary to indicate the start and end of a list. The sequential tape file uses the occurrence of a break in the sort key and/or the occurrence of a header record as a start indicator. In the case of chaining, with access keys or addresses, the end of a list may be indicated by the absence of a pointer to the next record.

If chaining is used, the pointer to the next entry in the list can be contained in the data record itself or in a table which contains the address or access key of all entries in the list (Figure 5-1). In addition, a list may be made symmetric (go both directions) by including the address or access key of both the next and prior entry in the list (Figure 5-2). Finally, the list is "headed" if each member of the list contains the address or access key of the owner or head of the list (Figure 5-2). Note that a list which is implemented as a table is implicitly headed and symmetric. The final form of a list is a ring structure in which the last member of the list contains the address or access key of the start (a table is implicitly a ring). The ring structure is more valuable

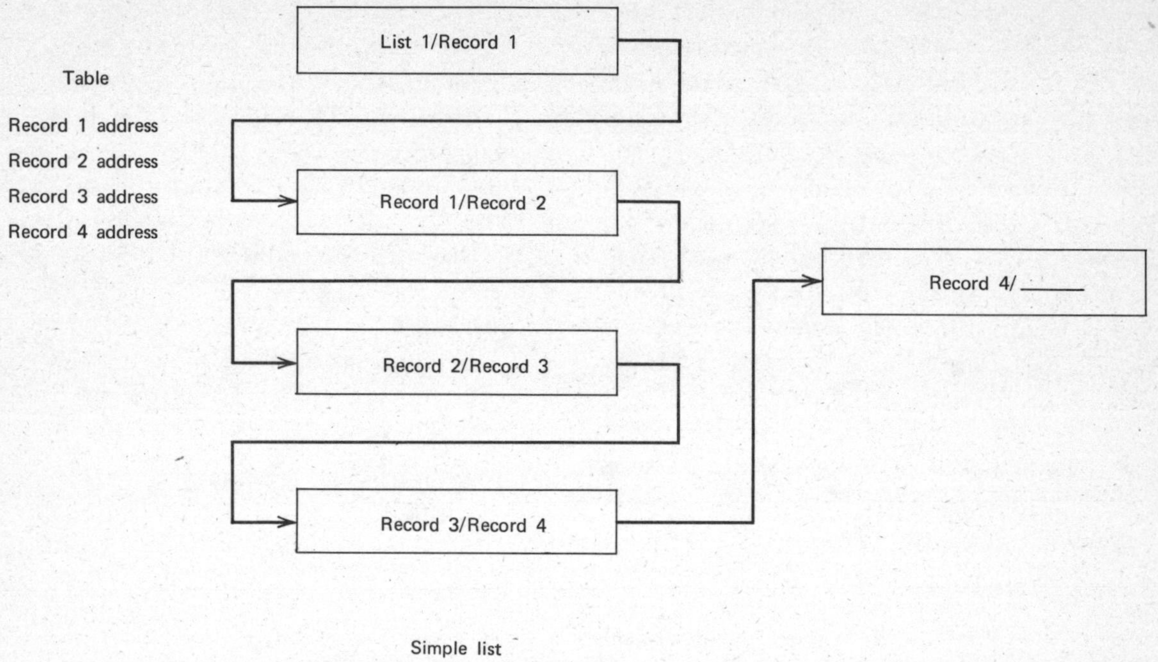

Figure 5-1 **Illustration of table and simple list.**

with a knotted list than it is with the simple list. Each of these results in the structure:

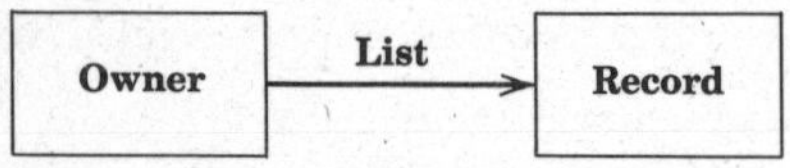

The knotted list structure is used to tie a single record into more than one list and is nothing more than cross/correlation. The knotted list can be implemented using more than one technique, but experience has shown that some form of ring structure is essential (either by heading, prior, pure ring, or table). The processing of a knotted list structure is in some ways analogous to driving in a strange city in which the following is true.

- The streets are all one way (sequential).
- The streets are labeled only at the city limits (head).
- Any given intersection may or may not permit turns.

In the context of the data base, an "intersection" exists only if the cross-correlation exists.

In terms of our previous examples of men, skills, and machines (Figure 5-3), each man represents an east-west street and each machine a north-south street. An intersection (skill) is defined if and only if it applies simultaneously to both the man and machines. Certainly we would not expect valid intersections to exist between all men and all machines. For the contents of each of the three records in a pure knotted list structure, see Figure 5-4.

An expansion of this concept is shown in Figure 5-1 for a table and simple list. Figure 5-2 illustrates the use of "pointers" in a headed symmetric list. If a knotted list is not used, the effect of the structure in Figure 5-1 can be achieved by creating either of the structures in Figure 5-2. Such

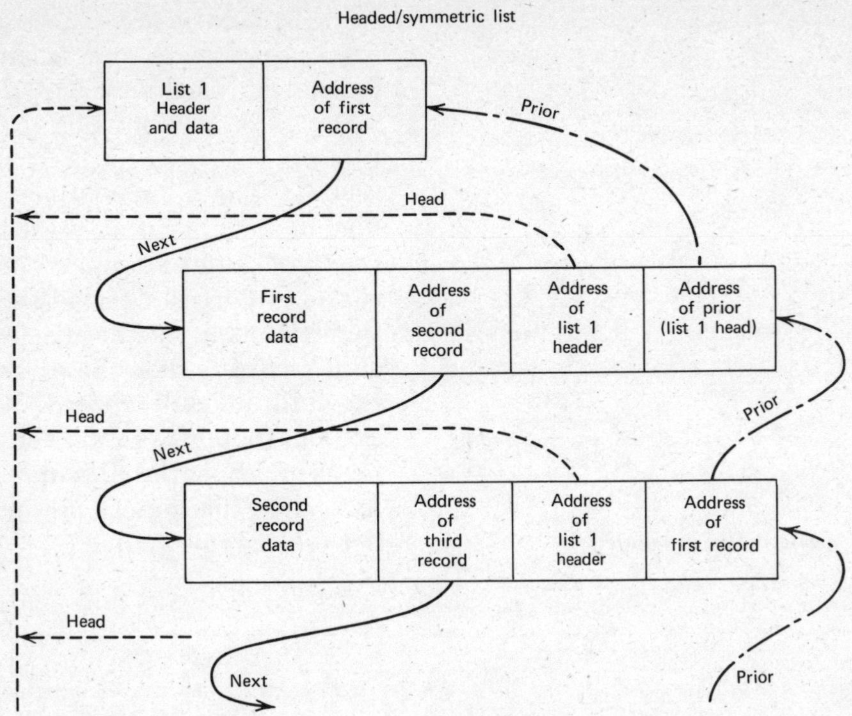

Figure 5-2 **Illustration of headed/symmetric list.**

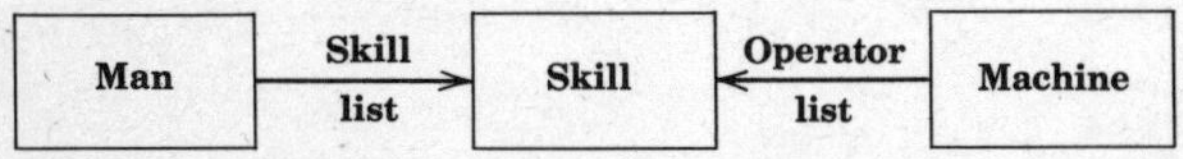

Figure 5-3 **Man/skill/machine example.**

an alternative creates duplicate records but does permit the use of simple list processing. In the first alternative, each machine **(machine)** heads a list of names of

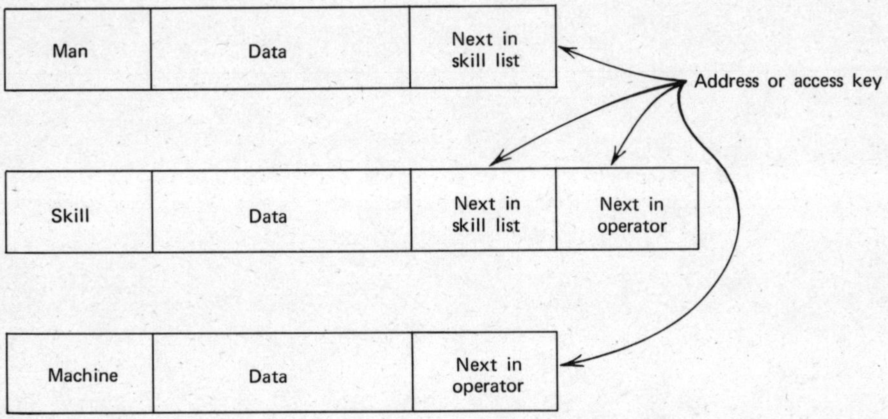

Figure 5-4 **Record layout for knotted list.**

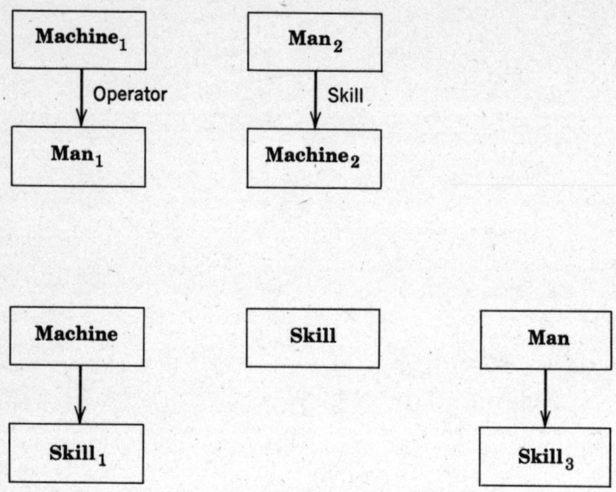

Figure 5-5 **Alternative to knotted list.**

men **(man)** who are qualified to operate that machine and each man **(man)** heads a list of machines **(machine)** which he is qualified to operate. The obvious problems of maintaining both lists is discussed in the next section. The second alternative uses three files or lists. Two of these are identical to the first alternative except that the lists contain addresses of the **skill** record rather than the name of the machine or man. The skill record is then the cross index to either the **skill**$_1$ or **skill**$_3$ record. Both alternatives are an attempt to retain the physical advantages of sequential files and, simultaneously, to realize the logical power of the knotted list (see Figure 5-5).

SECTION 6

Implementation–Physical/Logical Trade-Offs

The only design in the world that is physically and logically pure is that which is described by the computer manufacturer at the product announcement press conference. By the time the first piece of hardware is delivered, its design has been compromised more times than a "lady of pleasure" at the state fair.

The logical and physical techniques which have been described must now be converted into a deliverable package. The lofty principles of "nonredundant data," "total security," "an answer to any question," "simultaneous access," "reactive, time share, and batch," must be treated realistically. This section discusses the trade-offs which must be made and, more importantly, shows why they are necessary. The space/time trade-off is discussed in detail in addition to the frequently ignored (if I don't look, it won't hurt) utilization versus maintenance trade-off.

The problems of redundant data, data integrity, data security, updating of a community file, file segmentation, buffer management, data independence, and data base survival are examined in terms of their impact on implementation time and cost.

BASIC CONSIDERATIONS—A PERFORMANCE GOAL

The preceding sections have prepared the foundation for the logical design of a data base and the physical access techniques are arrayed before us. However, before we attack the problems of implementing a data base, it seems prudent to define first the problem and then the criteria which will be used to measure the success or failure of the solution. It is unfortunate but true that the program library is full of solutions in search of a problem, and systems that use a fire hose when an eye dropper would have been sufficient. Programmers, as a group, are often suspected of being compulsive innovators. It has also been suspected (probably by programmers) that data processing managers, as a group, "do not make waves" in an attempt to maintain the status quo.

In order to reconcile this dilemma, the programmers' creativity must be channeled by providing an appropriate statement of the real problem and not the superficial aspects. I suspect that all the "skeletons in the closet" of the program library are there because no one defined the real problem and, furthermore, no one ever defined standards of success. These same factors—lack of problem definition and lack of standards of evaluation—are even more acute in the field of data bases if for no other reason than the emotional appeal a data base has for management.

Assuming that the designer has the techniques and tools to design and implement a data base, he must have some sound basis for selecting among the alternatives and for specifying program logic. One of the first considerations is the definition of the customer, both short and long term. It must be decided early in the game who is going to pay the bill and who is going to determine success. The identification of the real customer reveals two things: first, it provides a great deal of insight into the kinds of things he should be doing with the data base; and second, it permits the designer to "feel his wallet." This last point is probably the most neglected of all the design tools available. When a customer describes what he wants he is probably reciting a list of all the latest "buzz" words and gossip from last month's *Datamation.* If the amount he expects to pay is very different than the amount the designer thinks the job is worth, then it is likely that the two are discussing two different problems. If the customer can be identified it is safe to expect that his needs and desires can be anticipated. In many cases, the customer is the least capable of specifying needs, not because he does not know them, but merely because he is unaware of what is available; a good system designer can provide valuable assistance.

If the customer has been identified and if an understanding regarding cost has been reached, the initial specification performance goals should be agreed upon. If the system is to use on-line terminals, the scope of the user's interaction with the system must be determined. Specifically, see the following:

- What functions can he perform?
- What limits are placed on access?
- What security measures are to be implemented?
- Are there restricted time periods?
- What is the tolerance of the system to error?

Obviously, the list is almost limitless. The point is to identify the role of the terminal both as a mode of operation and as a part of the system which will be built on the data base. It is always possible to tailor a system to respond rapidly to a terminal, but at the risk of degrading the performance of the system for other types of processing. For example, it is quite common to rebuild inverted files every time maintenance is performed. In such cases, the speed of the response characteristic is overriding. Whether this is good, depends on the performance goals of the customer. If the file is sufficiently large, and if it is an active file with a high level of maintenance activity, it may very well be a poor system even though it is fast.

In basic terms, the designer must determine and then create system performance elements which define the activity (store, change, delete), volume, and frequency for each kind of record in the data base. After these basic performance elements are defined, it is then necessary to determine the level of data base activity created by each program or subsystem. This last examination should indicate possible physical groupings of records in order to enhance its overall efficiency. It should be pointed out that while these performance considerations are important, they are often overemphasized. While all data bases are (or at least should be) designed with only the greatest of foresight, time will tell how they are actually used. Too many systems are built in response to yesterday's requirements. When a data base goes on line, the user's demands will rapidly shift toward selective retrieval and exception reporting on random time schedules and away from the periodic volume reporting currently in vogue. In fact, the "sacred cow" of collation sequence should disappear in a selective reporting environment (it may, in fact, be desirable to publish selective reports in a random sequence in order to encourage selectivity). Evaluation of the performance elements indicates:

- Desirable physical groupings of records
- Appropriate access methods
- Necessity to provide duplicate fields
- Desirability of data redundancy
- Restart and recovery procedures
- Physical groupings for security

Physical grouping of records is done either to reduce access time or to provide a measure of security. In many cases it is sufficient to recognize that the existence of a logical association indicates that physical proximity is also desirable. However, if a record is associated with two different kinds of records, some sort of compromise is required. In the case of the man-machine-skill arrangement, the skill record can be placed near the man, near the machine, or neither, but it cannot physically be near to both. This is analogous to requiring a single record in a tape file to exist simultaneously in two different sort sequences.

From an access standpoint, if the skill is placed near the machine, as shown by the double lined arrow, one access is sufficient to determine how many men are qualified to operate that machine. If it is necessary to explicitly identify them, then one additional access is required for each man. Figure 6-1 also implies that one access per skill is required to determine how many and/or what skills a man possesses. The placement in Figure 6-1 is probably the appropriate one for most applications.

If the performance goals placed speed of response before file space and maintenance, then it may be appropriate to split the structure of Figure 6-1 by duplicating the skill record (see Figure 6-2). If the structure of Figure 6-2 is employed, the basic data of man and machine are duplicated in the **skill**$_1$ and **skill**$_2$ records in order to equalize the speed of retrieval from either side. All the skills for a man can be found on the same access because they are physically located near the man. At the same

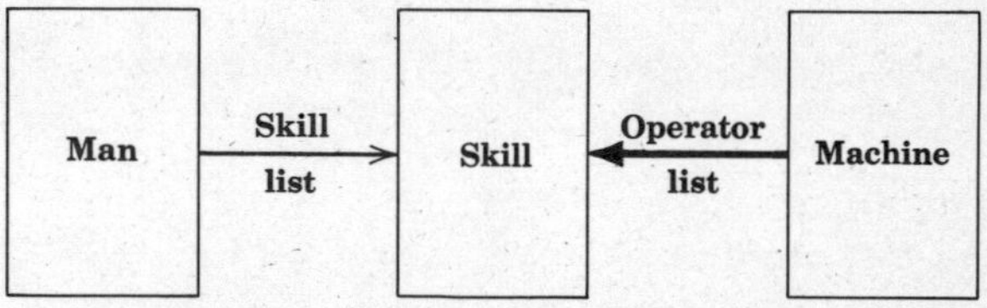

Figure 6-1 **Man-skill-machine structure.**

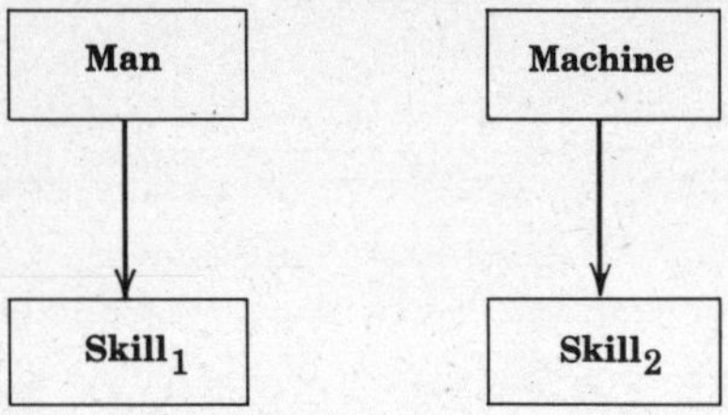

Figure 6-2 **Split file.**

time, all the men for a machine are found on the same access because of the proximity of the **$skill_2$** and their **machine** records.

Note the implications to maintenance. Since there is no direct structural tie between the two files, it is logically possible, with a split file, to enter a $skill_1$ for a nonexistent machine and, similarly, a $skill_2$ for a nonexistent man. More likely is the case of a man leaving the employment of the company; that is, the man record and all the $skill_1$ records are deleted, but for one reason or another, one or more of the corresponding **$skill_2$** records remain. When a direct tie exists, as in Figure 6-1, control is more positive. The split file of Figure 6-2 is the result of a space/time trade-off in which retrieval time is gained at the expense of space and at the expense of time used to maintain the file.

The second common area of space/time trade-off arises whenever a hierarchial structure is encountered. This commonly arises with financial data: costs, sales, or budgets. Consider briefly the fixed hierarchy of three levels, each with its own budget, as in Figure 6-3. Note that its logical structure is shown on the left and that it clearly and correctly implies that the section budget consists solely of the sum of all the budgets of the units which comprise that section, and similarly for the division. If a summary is maintained at each level in the hierarchy then the problem of maintenance becomes acute. Namely, if unit A13 is transferred from Section A1 to Section A2, the maintenance of summaries requires that the Section A1 total be reduced by 320 and probably the same for Division A; then a 320 increase must be made to both Division A and Section A2. If, however, the redundancy of data in the summary is not maintained, the transfer of unit A13 from Section A1 to A2 does not require extensive file maintenance. The trade-off in this case is a little more than time/space since it has a profound effect on data integrity. For our purposes, data integrity refers to the ability to analyze the same data from a multiplicity of directions and arrive at the same answer.

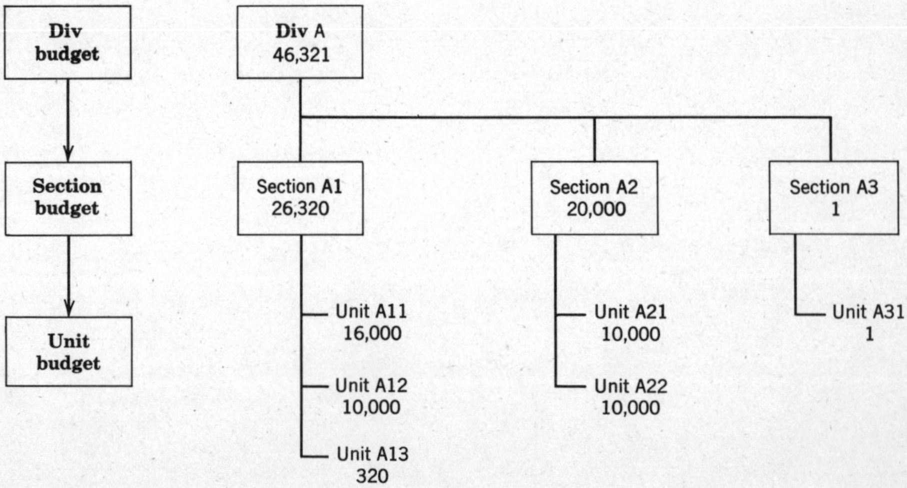

Figure 6-3 **Hierarchy and summary.**

If you have ever prepared a report of expenses by project and had the sum of all expenses balance to those summed by cost center, then you know that data integrity is sublime. The lack of integrity in data, for whatever reason, undermines the confidence that your customer has in your product. The trade-off here involves the use of structure versus procedure as the means of achieving integrity. The summary does increase the speed of response to a query, but at the same time drastically reduces the speed of maintenance and increases the complexity of the maintenance program.

FILE SECURITY

A data base is, and should remain, a community file. As long as the business enterprise depends upon its functional components for survival there is every reason to believe that it is necessary to maintain a policy which regards the data base as a public file available to all members of the community, that is, the business. It would, therefore, seem reasonable to assume that access to the file, and hence its security, should be determined, permitted, and controlled on the basis of "community good." In practical terms, this means that access to the file for the purpose of modifying its contents should be restricted severely. These restrictions are necessary for a variety of reasons but most importantly to

- Protect the integrity of the data (it is very unlikely that any one user of the community file is aware of the effect that a change in data base content can have on the other users).
- Maintain reasonable standards of control and audit (it is obviously undesirable to permit casual changes to data which describe the actual performance of the enterprise).
- Protect the sensitive corporate data from unauthorized exposure (it is unreasonable to open up salary information, for example, to everyone).
- Protect proprietary information.

Security of data, both to protect it from accidental and unauthorized tampering and from unauthorized disclosure, becomes more difficult with each attempt to make the data base more useful. If the data base and its supporting systems are restricted to the controlled environment of batch processing, the problem of security is relatively easy to accept. If it is opened up to include remote batch (input/output from remotely located devices), then practical security is achieved by controlling access to the data base. The next step in achieving usefulness is, of course, interactive access which presents the greatest complexity in providing adequate security.

An extremely powerful and useful technique for ensuring selective protection of sensitive data such as technical, proprietary, and/or personnel data is the use of physical separation of these data from the rest of the data base. Such physical separation is accomplished by assigning the record-types which contain such sensitive data to a separate, and perhaps a removable, device. For example, it is possible to create a structure as shown in Figure 6-4. In such

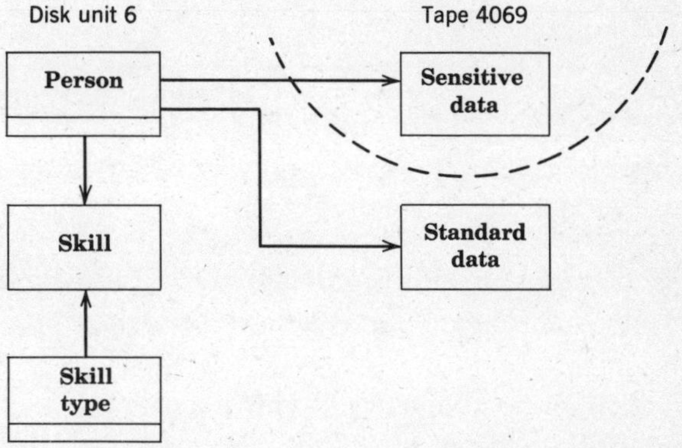

Figure 6-4 **Security through physical allocation.**

a case, it is desirable to maintain immediate access to a person's personnel data in order to fulfill the normal day-to-day problems of resource allocation. The standard data, such as home address and education, are open (unclassified or nonconfidential) knowledge within the company. Sensitive data, such as salary and medical data, are available only on a controlled, and probably batch mode basis.

The use of physical separation to provide protection is an extension to a technique which applies to any data storage device—namely, if you intend to restrict it, do not define it. If two programs are to use the same tape file, and certain fields are to be defined as to size only (FILLER in Cobol), there is no way for the user to address these fields directly. It is conceded that even an incompetent can rename the field to examine its value, but unless he knows precisely its form and meaning, it is probably unintelligible. In a multiple record data base (about 24 different record types) which is meant to serve a community of diverse users, such a simple technique as incomplete description is extremely valuable.

If the incomplete description concept is extended to include the program itself, rather than just the data base, a significant measure of security is obtained. This is equivalent to providing the user with a set of tools that will perform only a limited number of tasks. In a limited way, commercial time-sharing service provides the user with a number of basic functions which can be combined in any manner he wishes. But significantly, the system will respond only to the defined functions. In this way, the system and the other users are protected. This technique relies on the user's ignorance of the existence of, and access to, other programs.

It is possible to provide lock and key controls both physically at the terminal and logically through password and identification schemes which are used during sign-on, program call, file access, and at the record and field level. A level of security can be achieved at the record and field level if the user-identification (user-id) and/or password is incorporated into the access key. Furthermore, if this portion of the access key is always initialized by the system, based on the user-id, it will be impossible for a user to cross user-id boundaries.

Perhaps the most realistic method of protection is a reliance on the functional knowledge of the legitimate user and the "snooper's" corresponding lack of knowledge. By this presence, or lack, of knowledge it is implied that the detailed structure and content are foreign to the "snooper" and, at the same time, quite familiar to the legitimate user. This is especially true if data redundancy is minimized. Consider the example of the budgets used earlier in the section (Figure 6-3). If no summary data are maintained, the "snooper" would be required to traverse successfully a strange organizational structure in order to obtain a Division budget. This is a form of protection.

It should be obvious that security of the data base is achievable in a variety of ways. Note that each additional measure taken in the name of security reduces the usefulness of the data base. Its security problems are solved most effectively by exercising security at the point of file access which is the program. This, coupled with the relative absence of summary or redundant data, results in a reasonable compromise between utility and secrecy.

INPUT-OUTPUT CONTROL

The use of mass storage devices in a system oriented to a data base introduces a new dimension to the problems of managing the flow of data between core and the slower devices. It would seem safe to assert that there are no systems in existence today which do not buffer their input/output operations in some manner. With older and more conventional sequentially accessed files it is common (if not standard) to look ahead. Specifically it is normal to double buffer such that the inactive buffer can be emptied (output) or refreshed (input) while the active buffer is being used. This technique is valid only because there is almost an absolute certainty as to the address of the next block which will be required for processing.

This certainty evaporates as soon as selective processing is encountered. Selective processing by its very nature is random and, as such, there are few valid methods to predict which block will be "next." In addition, the tidiness of input and output files has disappeared; there is only the data base, which is simultaneously input and output.

The data base does, during its use, provide dynamic criteria for managing its own buffers. Note that even though the sequential certainty of buffer management has gone, the requirement for buffers has increased. A buffer is nothing more than a core image of a physical record from the file. The question of how many buffers should be provided depends on the structure of the data base and a specific application. If all the processing for a particular application uses but one record type, it is quite likely that one or two buffers will be sufficient (note that each level of indexing in an indexed sequential implementation is equivalent to another record type). If, on the other hand, a particular application is processing five or six different record types which are not normally physically close, as many as 10 or 15 buffers may be desirable. The point is that if a given block or physical record will be required in the immediate future, do not let it escape.

The precise method of handling buffers is most likely determined by the manufacturer of your machine. The technique following is discussed in order to provide insight into buffering, and not as a standard. This scheme is based entirely on a notion of subjective probability which says that the block which was just referenced (either accessed in mass storage or in core) is most likely to be accessed next. Thus the buffers are treated as a push down stack, with the top being the block just referenced and the one on the bottom being the oldest, and hence the least likely to be called. When a new block is accessed, it will go to the top of the stack and physically occupy the space held by the one previously on the bottom.

Note that if the block on the bottom of the stack contains any modifications whatsoever (new records added or old records changed or deleted), it must be written back to mass storage prior to being replaced by a new block. This suggests that a modified block is worth twice as much as a block which has not been changed; hence there is a criterion, other than time since last reference, for aging blocks in the buffer. As usual a user has intelligence at his disposal that could improve system performance through selective "aging" of buffers; for example, if he knows, once and for all, that he is finished with a particular block, the system can overlap its write back, if necessary, with computation.

FILE PROTECTION AND RECOVERY

The security provided by the "father" and "grandfather" copies of the master files is obsolete the day that the data base is installed. The master files of the sequential systems represented the business at fixed and arbitrary points of time. The data base, on the other hand, is normally dynamic in that it is updated as soon as data become available, not at arbitrary points in time.

A data base is sufficiently large to economically bar its resurrection through complete regeneration even if such regeneration was physically possible. As the size of data bases and mass storage devices increases, the designer must realistically face the problems of recovery.

The most obvious and familiar technique periodically produces a duplicate of the data base on magnetic tape. This security copy becomes the "father" copy of the data base. Recovery can be accomplished by reloading from tape and rerunning all of the transactions from the last period. Before accepting this method of recovery, remember that there are physical devices on the market with capacities approaching one billion characters and that these devices may require up to 5 hours to dump and another 5 hours to reload. This means that almost a whole shift is lost for copy alone.

A second alternative involves the use of a journal file to record the changes to the data base as they occur. The problem of recovery is then reduced to restoring the processed changes rather than rerunning each individual transaction. But how does one recover in the absence of transactions? One obvious technique would be to copy each record image at the time that it is either stored, altered, or deleted. If such images are serially indexed, it is possible to restore the data base by restoring only the effects of the changes; thereby bypassing the intervening processing. The deleted records are the "fly in the ointment" with their post-processing images imaginary at best.

The recording of physical record images is an attractive alternative to recording at the logical record level. While a physical record may be void (i.e., it contains no logical records), it always exists. If buffering is performed at the physical record level, it is not only sensible but convenient to journalize changes in physical records. Thus it is sufficient to sort the journal file by physical record and serial number and reload only the latest image of each altered block.

So far we have managed to cope with the problem of recovery from mechanical failure, that is, recovery by bringing the data base up-to-date. There is, however, an equally serious, logical failure which occurs as the result of program error, bad data, and so on. In order to recover from a logical error, it is possible to record, on the journal file, both before and after images of physical records which are changed. In order to recover a file which may be accessed by more than one user, it is necessary to tag the before and after images not only by sequence number (perhaps real time) but also by job number. Recovery from a logical error is then accomplished by reloading the affected before block images.

Journalization of physical record activity provides a systematic method for mechanical recovery. It is also prudent to consider the potential savings in recovery time that can be obtained through physical segmentation of the data base into subfiles. While such subfiling may be useful from an efficiency or security standpoint, it is equally valuable as a means of facilitating the recovery of a compromised data base. The decision as to distribution of record types across devices should be based on the following considerations:

- The most active record-types should reside on the fastest available device.
- The least active record should be relegated to the slowest devices.
- The most critical records should reside on the fast devices.

- The rarest records (i.e., not many in the data base) could be on the fast devices.

The fast device is most likely to be the easiest to recover and/or save in terms of the number of channels, relatively low storage capacity, and time. The critical records are those whose nonavailability would cause system shutdown. By collecting the rarest records, it is possible to reduce the effort required to restore these records in the event of a failure. Regardless of the specific techniques used to facilitate recovery, it pays to plan ahead. Examine the expected frequency of activity of each record type and the impact that the record has on the system; then plan the recovery strategy accordingly.

SECTION 7

Efficiency–The Thinking Man's Design

All of the tools needed to implement a data base, which is technically and logically sufficient, have now been assembled. As a matter of fact, enough of these tools have been accumulated to permit more than one physical implementation of the same logical data base. The fact that it is possible to realize more than one implementation of the same logical structure introduces the potential for either time or space savings through the consideration of efficiency.

This section is directed to the disagreeable task of thinking —or more appropriately, the application of common sense. Specific attention is directed to the use of preprocessing and/or post-processing of data; the use of sequential and random (selective) processing; the criteria for selecting among various addressing techniques (dictionary, physical sequential, logical sequential, layered indices, etc.); the relative roles of unanticipated query languages and parameter-driven inquiry; the role of security and utility; speed of retrieval, and so on. Each of these factors is discussed in terms of physical devices, interpretive software, and host languages. These factors are emphasized through the use of examples and analysis.

SUPPLEMENTAL PROCESSING

In the past, many techniques have been employed which were intended to make like easier for the programmer. Such techniques will normally permit more efficient processing of information. But what constitutes efficiency? In the days of UNIVAC I and the 650's, efficiency was speed measured in terms of elapsed time. The programmer had a limited resource (time) at his disposal; since he tied up the entire machine every time he began to process, elapsed time was the direct measure of cost.

As the state of the art advanced, the multiprogrammed computer system was introduced; and, as operating systems were shaken down, shared access has become the accepted standard of processing. Unfortunately, shared access confused our heretofore simplistic measure of efficiency. Since many users can simultaneously share the resources of the information processing system, it is only fair to allocate the cost of the used resources, as opposed to the older base of elapsed time. This implies that it is possible to assign the cost of core, cpu time, channel time, tape transports, mass storage, and the other peripherals. While different manufacturers may use different billing algorithms, they have all recognized that usage should be billed not on elapsed time, but rather on actual resources consumed (and hence denied to others). In such an environment, a possible definition of efficiency is based on minimum cost: if the billing algorithm is, in fact, realistic, cost is, perhaps, the only acceptable measure of efficiency.

If two systems fulfill absolutely the same performance requirements, then the one which is the least expensive to operate is the most efficient. Unfortunately, it is usually impossible to achieve agreement on absolute performance since such requirements are usually evaluated relative to cost.

There are several approaches to the problem of minimizing total operating cost. Within the environment of sequential processing, it is standard practice to accumulate transactions over a period of time, sort the transactions into the same sequence as the master file, and then perform update by merging the old master file and the transaction file. Because our master file is now maintained on a random access, mass storage device, we should not forget all the hard-learned lessons of sequential processing. While preprocessing was mandatory with sequential files, it is now necessary to determine when such preprocessing is worthwhile. The basic consideration in evaluating the desirability of preprocessing is "how much."

The cost of processing random transactions, as opposed to that of processing batched transactions, is determined almost entirely by the number of accesses to the mass storage device. The theoretical maximum number of times a data base should be accessed physically is (read only) the number of physical records (blocks) in the data base, and for updating, twice the number of blocks (once to read and once to write back). Obviously, this limit implies a certain type of file structure; namely, that of a tree.

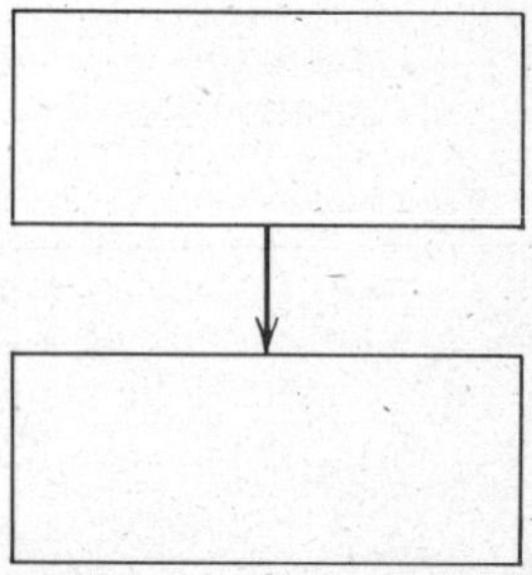

If cross indexing is present and required, the limit becomes less precise but is proportional to the number of physical records in the data base, the number of cross indices, and the number of logical records involved.

For example, the structure below has two dimensions of indexing, by **man** and by **machine.**

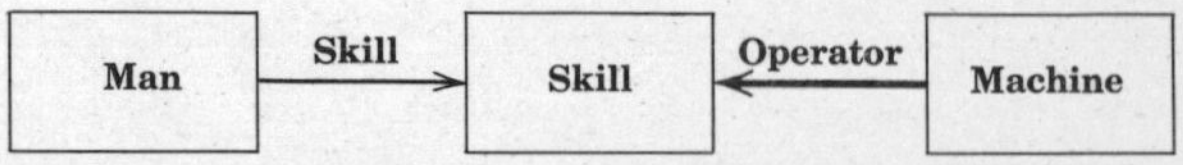

Since in a knotted list, the **skill** record exists only once, it can be physically near only one of its "owners," in this case, **machine.** Therefore, it follows that the maintenance of **skill** records can be optimized for only one of its two indices, simply because each of the set classes is analogous to a separate sequential file. The choice of sequence is based on several factors, but primarily on the relative physical span of these two record types. If, for example, the **machine** records are contained within a span of 30 physical records, but the **man** records covered a span of 60, it is advantageous to place the transactions into machine sequence. It is important to realize that

- If the transactions are sorted by machine, the corresponding references to man are random.
- If the transactions are sorted by man, the corresponding references to machine are random.

For example, it is highly unlikely to expect that two consecutive transactions, sorted by machine, would involve either the same man or even two man records within the same physical record.

The decision to preprocess (sort) the transaction records must be based on the cost of sorting as opposed to the expected additional cost of random processing. Assume the following parameters:

- 300 man records over 60 physical records (blocks)
- 200 machine records over 90 blocks
- 90 skill records over 90 blocks

Then the expected number of any one record type on a block is

$300/60 = 5$ for the man record
$200/90 = 2.22$ for the machine record
$900/90 = 10$ for the skill record

For example, if 10 transactions are to be processed, then the probability of encountering two transactions involving the same block is

$$p \cong (10/90)^2 \cong (.111)^2 \simeq .01$$

This indicates that it is a random process. But if there are as few as 90 transactions, then one transaction per block is expected—very close to a sequential process. The actual distribution of logical records to a block, assuming randomness, is Poissoin. The probability of successive transactions applying to a given block is binomial. For example, the probability of having at least one transaction on a block is .65; at least two, .26; at least three, .07; at least four, .01; and the probability that a block will not be accessed is approximately .35. Thus for the case of 90 transactions, we would expect to have about 59 (90 times .65) accesses. If the cost of presorting the transactions is less than the cost of the extra 31 accesses, then sort. If, for example, 180 transactions were processed, the unsorted would require 180 accesses, while 79 are expected if they are sorted. As the number of transactions increases, the number of accesses approaches 90, or the number of blocks.

So much for the numbers game; preprocess only if the expected savings exceed the additional cost. The second point to be made is that the preprocessing (sorting in the previous example) places transactions in the physical sequence of mass storage, which may be the same as the collation sequence. This situation can be expected if a calculation technique for accessing records is employed. Note, also, that if indexed sequential is used, the number of accesses in the example must be multiplied by the number of levels of indexing.

Sorting is one of several items in the bag of efficiency tricks. Another form of supplemental processing is editing. Editing can take many forms and can be used during several different stages of processing. The simplest form of editing involves a check to ensure that all of the required data fields are present on the input document. Next, it is possible to check the nature of the data in light of a transaction code; and finally, it is possible to verify the validity and consistency of actual data values prior to storing records. As with sorting, such editing has value only if it costs less than the processing of invalid data.

Too often, efficiency is measured only in terms of input processing. In many cases, the internal and terminal aspects are forgotten. Internally, do not initiate a search for anything you may already have. In most direct-access processing, 50 percent or more of the processing and mass storage I/O is done solely for the purpose of "positioning." "Positioning" is the act of finding the owner of a specific list in order to process each of its members in turn. If you have reason to expect that you are dealing, even twice, with the same list, stop, and consider the cost of checking every time, as compared to the cost of needlessly repositioning.

Note that the "list" need not be an explicit user designed structure, but rather may be the method of implementation chosen by the user's supplier of software. In fact, it is probably safe to say that the only nonlist software implementation for random access mass storage is direct addressing (physical) at the record level. Processing an indexed sequential implementation is in reality list processing within the indices and within the physical record.

As with input processing, terminal processing is often a fruitful area of searching for inefficiencies. Reporting on a periodic basis is normally a batch process in which every item in the data base is examined but not necessarily extracted. Reporting is a sequential process and usually involves the reporting of the same data in several different sort sequences. It may be that the physical sequence of records on the mass storage device does not coincide with any of the reporting sequences. In such cases, the task of efficiently reporting is reducible to the generation of one or more sequential files, which can be repeatedly sorted into the desired sequences. The decision to extract in physical sequence, as opposed to logical sequence, should be made on the same basis as was preprocessing—namely cost.

LOGICAL ORGANIZATION

From a purely logical point of view, the two structures in Figure 7-1 are identical. The difference occurs in the method of accessing the **man** and the **machine.** Access to **skill** is dependent upon the other two record types. For the moment, underlining implies a directly accessible record, either by calculation or by knowledge of its address. The top portion of Figure 7-1 represents an indexed sequential access. As a practical matter, an attempt to retrieve any specific man record can be expected to require at least three accesses (read three physical records) using the indexed sequential access and at least one access using either the calculated or the "known ad-

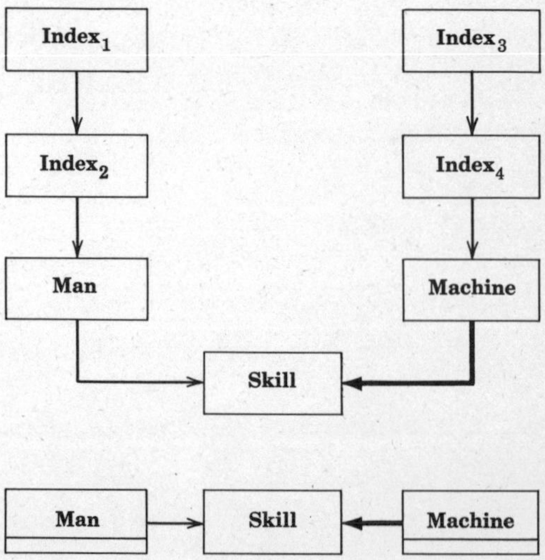

Figure 7-1 **Equivalent structures.**

dress" technique. This example correctly implies that, for selective processing, the structure in the lower half of Figure 7-1 is more efficient. However, if the volume of retrieval increases such that having accessed a given physical record, at least three of its logical records will be used, then the two structures are equally efficient. If it is important to preserve any intelligence in number; for example, if the fact that two numbers or identifiers are close in the collation sequence is significant, then indexed sequential is logically more valuable than calculated access. For example, if the identifier of the **man** record (i.e., the access key) is **name**, and if it is necessary to locate all men whose last name is Smith, then there is intelligence in the "nearness" of identifiers, and indexed sequential access is preferable.

Unfortunately, it is usually impossible to guarantee that a data base will be used in only one manner. There is no reason why a structure cannot accommodate more than one method of access. Such a structure could result by providing two methods of access to the basic record of our **man** and **machine** example; specifically, indexed sequential, and calculated. In a knotted list processor, this presents no problem, although it may be more cumbersome with other processing techniques. For example, the basic records may be stored physically using calculation and at the same time, a separate file of abbreviated records may be created and organized using indexed sequential. This abbreviated record could contain the physical address of the full data record in the calculated random file.

PROCESSING APPROACH

There are five basic processes which will be used during the life of a data base. The problems of each of these processes, in the light of efficiency, are sufficiently different to warrant some modest consideration.

The first basic process is the initial creation or load. The load process is characterized by a relatively high volume of transactions in which a natural hierarchy of record-types exists; that is, it is necessary to establish the header before any trailers are established. Thus in the **man/skill/machine** example, it is desirable to establish all of the **man/machine** records prior to attempting to load the **skill** records. This implies that the load of these three types of records breaks down into a natural sequence of operations. Assume that we currently possess two master files on tape: the first is essentially the **skills** list, which is maintained in sequence by man; the second, the **operator** list by machine. If the data on the two master files are totally redundant and believed to be consistent, then either one of the tapes can be discarded. However, the files are probably inconsistent and furthermore, the **skill** file would normally contain more man data than the operator file. In order to minimize accesses, first sort the **skill** file into the physical disk sequence and then store all the **man** records. Second, sort the **operator** file into eventual **machine** record sequence and store the **machine** record and each of its associated **skill** records. If a **skill** record is encountered in the **operator** file for which no **man** record exists, do not store it. This set of steps not only minimizes the number of physical accesses, but also is useful in creating a data base whose records are physically sorted when the physical and collation sequences (as in indexed sequential) are identical.

The next two types of processing are used to add, change, and remove data base records. The distinction between the two types is based on volume. The term maintenance is restricted to low volume (selective) changes while update is used to refer to higher volume (batched) changes. In some cases, the only distinction between the two will be preprocessing while in others there will be significant differences. The choice between the two is based on the ratio of the number of transactions to the number of physical records (blocks). If this ratio is less than 1, then the changes to the data base are random and it is efficient to treat each transaction as independent. If, however, the ratio is greater than 1 (update) it is efficient to preprocess such that the transactions are placed in their physical sequence of the mass storage device. The sole intent of such processing is to ensure a minimum number of physical accesses.

The last two types of processing deal with reporting. As with data base maintenance, the distinction is one of volume. If the expected number of physical reads is small compared to the total number of blocks, then the reporting is truly selective. One possible estimate of the number of physical reads is the number of owner records needed to complete the report. Going back to the example in Figure 7-1, the lower illustration would require approximately one access to get the **machine** record and all of its **skill** records, and one additional access to get the **man** associated with each of the **skills.** In a two-dimensional situation, as in Figure 7-1, a fair estimate is $n + 1$ accesses for each **machine** where n is the average number of **skills** per **machine.** If the upper half of Figure 7-1 is used, then this number may become as much as a $3(n + 1)$, unless, of course, totally redundant data are maintained in the **skill** record.

If the expected number of accesses approaches twice the number of physical blocks of this portion of the data base, it is time to strip the file and create a sequential file. This is achieved by transferring a copy or extract of each data base record to tape, and then sorting by access key and record type. Logically, the process consists of collapsing the three record-type file into two types as shown in the following.

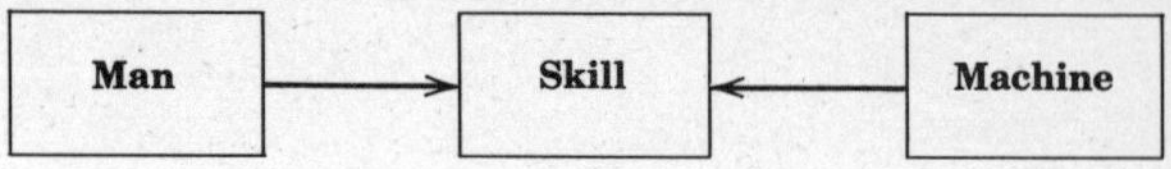

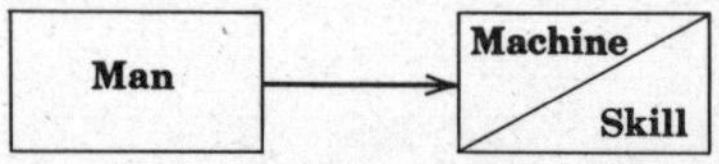

The new **machine skill** record contains redundantly all of the data contained in both the **skill** and **machine** records, a field for record type, and a field containing the access key of the **man** record (that **man** record which was the owner of the **skill** record in the data base). The sort then effectively creates a one record-type file as the following:

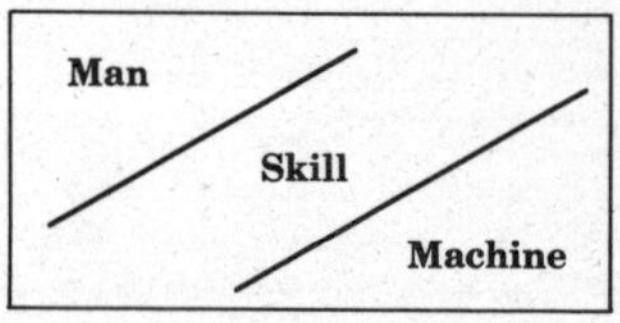

This can be sorted repeatedly to provide enough paper to bury either the shop steward or the foreman.

The fact that the data base was stripped does not imply that it should not have been created in the first place, but, rather, that it is often prudent to think first and then act: use the mode of processing which is most efficient for the task at hand. While the entire file was stripped in this case, the normal situation is to strip those portions (containing logically limited sets of record types) which would otherwise require excessive number of physical reads. The basic premises on which the file was structured remain valid; namely, to encourage selective processing, to reduce redundancy, and to enhance the quality of information by the elimination and prevention of inconsistent data. In many cases, the value of the data base as an active processing file is overshadowed by its value as a method of organizing and maintaining data.

LOGICAL VERSUS PHYSICAL ADDRESSING

Thus far we have discussed seriously only two kinds of logical addressing: computation and indexed sequential. While the method of addressing can be indicated on a structure diagram, as in Figure 7-1, this is not normal. In many cases, the method of addressing is either totally beyond the control of the designer and/or programmer or he chooses to ignore the alternatives which are available to him.

There are three kinds of addressing which can exist within a system. First, there is a physical address which is directly interpreted as a physical location within the mass storage device. This physical address may completely specify the necessary arguments for an assembly language I/O instruction. Second, there is a logical address from which the software is capable of determining a physical address. Finally, there is an access key, from which either a logical or physical address can be determined.

Consider briefly the characteristics of logical addressing. First, it will normally be sufficient to use a maximum of one word (24 to 36 bits) for a logical address. Second, once assigned, logical addresses should remain unchanged even though the record itself may have been physically moved. Third, a logical address contains an implicit reference to the physical record or block and some further breakdown identifying the logical record within its assigned block. Fourth, logical addresses must be unique: that is, a logical address cannot refer to two or more different physical locations. Fifth, logical addresses should be assigned such that two or more logical addresses do not refer to the same physical addresses (i.e., synonyms). Sixth, the logical address of a record uniquely identifies the record; that is, it is a unique record identifier and is, therefore, logically equivalent to its access key even though it may be shorter. Seventh, if the "known address" method is used to access a record, it is the logical address which should be used.

Logical addressing permits the designer to obtain the benefits of device independence. Since the logical address does not contain a device type or address, the data base can reside on any direct access media and still be operable. In fact, by copying from one device to another, a data base can be run on more than one device. Logical addressing is significant as a method of spreading a data base across multiple devices while maintaining only a single logical addressing scheme. This removes any artificial restrictions placed on the user due to the physical limitations of a particular mass storage device. It also permits the user to place his high utilization portions of the data base on the high speed units, and the more voluminous and less frequently accessed data on slower bulk storage units.

The techniques for converting logical to physical addresses are numerous. Typical approaches involve computation, table look-up, and segmentation. Pure linear computation implies a homogeneity of device addressing and contiguous storage across all devices. Computation would take all or part of the logical address to determine: the device number, block within device, and record within block either absolutely or relative to some base. Table look-up involves either a binary or an exhaustive search of the table to determine the physical address which corresponds to the logical address. Such tables can be layered to speed the search. For example, the highest level table may indicate the next table to look in, and the second, the third, and so on, until at the bottom level an entry is found for every logical address for which a record exists. It is obvious that while such tables can be constructed for use in a retrieve-only situation but they may become extremely cumbersome when it is necessary to insert records into the data base.

Segmentation is a compromise between the table look-up and computation techniques. First, it contains only one table whose entries contain the following:

- The range of admissible logical addresses
- The base address for this segment
- The computational rule for determining block within device and position within block

While complete tabularization verified that a record existed before physical access, the physical presence of a specific logical address can be determined in segmentation only by actually accessing the data base.

The final type of addressing records is through the use of access keys. This is nothing more than determining an address (physical or logical) based on the value of a data field. In the terms of a calculated access record, this involves the use of an algorithm which will convert the value of the data field into a valid address. Indexed sequential relies on searching a sorted list to determine the address of a record.

Typically, a set of tables (shown in Figure 7-1 as **index$_1$** and **index$_2$**) are created and maintained. Within the structure of Figure 7-1, the user would supply a value for the access key. Either the system or the user would then search through the **index$_1$** records until one was found which contained within its range the value being sought. Having found the correct **index$_1$** record, a search of **index$_2$** records, which it owns, would be made until the one was found which contained the value of the access key within its range. Finally, a search would be made of the **man** records which are "owned" by that **index$_2$** record. If there were 27,000 **man** records within our file, it would be desirable to create 30 **index$_1$** records each owning 30 **index$_2$** records (900 in all) and each of these, owning 30 **man** records, for a total of 27,000 records. Any search for a specific **man**, selected at random, would involve, on the average, the accessing of 15½ records at each level for a total of 46.5 records. Because such records will normally be clustered by level and by owner on the mass storage device, only three or four physical reads would be expected.

There are two ways to handle the bottom level. The first is to have the actual data records sorted on the disk such that the bottom level search is physical. Thus we deal with actual addresses only. If this technique is used, the number of disk reads is expected to be somewhat larger than the one or two mentioned in the previous paragraph (depending on physical block size and the number of logical records per block). With such a sequential/sequential organization, the following is true:

- It is necessary to move physically records in order to insert a new record, or to adjust the position of an existing record due to a change in its data value. Depending upon the relative position within a block, this may involve significant amounts of data.
- Records with duplicate values of access key require special attention.
- Reorganization of the data base is straightforward, since addressing is based entirely on access key.
- Cross-referencing is obtainable only through the use of access keys which may increase, drastically, the number of accesses.

A possible alternative to the sequential/

sequential (i.e., the records are logically and physically sequential) is to replace the physical record with its address. Since the address and access key are considerably shorter than the whole record, it is obvious that the bottom level (the group of 30 records in our example) can be accessed with a single physical read, and the desired record with an additional access. This is known as sequential/random. The records are addressed sequentially (i.e., logically) but are physically placed at random.

Finally, if logical addressing is to be used, the assignment of such address must have an intelligent correlation to the corresponding physical address if any type of supplemental processing is to be meaningful. Specifically, if a set of logical addresses are sorted, it is necessary that the corresponding physical addresses also be sorted.

WHISTLES AND BELLS

The preceding considerations of efficiency were based entirely on the relatively sound ground of reason and technology. This subsection is an attempt to discuss the more emotional aspects of efficiency as they apply to the human interface. From a technical standpoint, the use of a computer by a man at a terminal device is, at best, an offensive abuse of a valuable and scarce resource. If the operating system was designed to ignore the interactive terminal until it is idle, then the terminal becomes only slightly less offensive. However, if such an approach is taken, then the terminal would have no value as an interactive device and would be marginal as a device for initiating batch jobs.

Unfortunately, the processor and its associated peripherals cannot be isolated from the environment of which it is, at best, an expensive but minor member. The total information processing system includes, as an integral part, those people who must interact with it, either as generators of source documents and control parameters, or as users of the output. While the processor and operating system may "spin their collective wheels" waiting for input from a teletype (or some other equally slow device), the net effect of interactive computation should be either reduced net cost of operating the business, or an effective increase in value (perhaps greater profit) of the business. It may cost less in terms of materials, to produce a 120-page inventory report every week than to have 30 selective inquiries per day in an interactive mode, but it is likely that those 30 selective queries either reduced the cost of labor of plowing through a report which is by definition out of date, or either increased revenue or reduced material cost through action based on timely and pertinent data.

The presence of a structured data base on mass storage encourages the use of selective inquiry. The problem for the system designer is one of determining an efficient approach to random selective processing. It is axiomatic that the more difficult a system is to use, the more efficient it is likely to be. Of the several approaches to servicing the interactive and/or selective processing user, the two broad categories of unanticipated query and parameter structure cover the field. Basically, a structured, parameter-driven, query system will permit answers only to those queries which the system designer either knew how to solve or decided were significant. Such systems rely on the user to identify the question (one of several permissible), and then to supply the parameters necessary to select the data. This is equivalent to setting up a subroutine call and the corresponding argument list. It is normal to use special symbols as delimiters between fields. A parameter system uses an extremely efficient approach to selective processing for those situations in which the same kind of question is repeatedly asked—the only distinction between questions being the actual data valves (such as customer number, part number) used to select records.

Unanticipated query systems are characterized by a less rigidly structured syntax and less efficient processing compared to the parameter query. They do, on the other hand, permit greater freedom in the types of questions that can be structured and in the amount and form of the criteria used to select records for processing. It appears that every data base should have both kinds of systems. The parameter-driven systems will flourish because they simultaneously appeal to the DP professional on the basis of efficiency and to the user on the basis of usefulness. There are some cynics in this business who suspect that parameter systems are popular with users because of their status value—"my branch's system is better than yours.'' The unanticipated query should appeal to the free thinkers in the office since it is usually free form and does not restrict the user (meaning he does not have to think), and, at the same time, it provides a means of responding quickly to specific requests for information. If any one request is asked frequently, it can then be incorporated into the parameter system on a relatively leisurely schedule.

Regardless of the approach taken to facilitate selective processing, be assured that all users are unreasonable, unpredictable, and contradictory. First, protect the system from the user. Do not try to outguess the user and do not be forgiving of syntax errors. If the user's intention was misinterpreted, the incorrect answers which may be returned will not only be an irritant, but also they may cause the customer to make a costly mistake.

A user will demand that any selective processing system be user-oriented, which usually means that he is intimidated by keypunch machines and teletypes, or that he cannot spell; therefore, mysterious symbols that no one else understands are better. He will disclaim (sometimes correctly) any knowledge of computers and will insist that the system lead him step-by-step to a correct answer. In fact he will quickly become intolerant to any unnecessary chit chat from the terminal or any superfluous input. The only answer is to assume that a user is knowledgeable and to provide assistance on request or in the event of error.

Regardless of type, selective retrieval capability is enhanced by the amount and number of cross-classifications. Each classification is nothing more than an access key. Recalling the claims file example of Section 3, there were five types of classification for each claim in addition to access by claim number. As an example, assume that there are 10,000 claim folders in the file and that there are then:

- 2500 claims in each drawer
- 250 claims for each divider
- 9000 ''insured'' records
- 11,000 ''claimant'' records
- 30 ''coverage'' records
- 50 ''accident'' records
- 3 ''hot'' records

If the claims are evenly distributed among each category within a class (an average of 1.1 claims per insured record, or one claim per claimant, etc.) then the selectivity of each class can be ranked as in Table 7-1.

Table 7-1
Relative Selectivity of Classes of Data

Class	Selectivity
Claim number	10,000
Claimant	11,000
Insured	9,000
Accident	50
Divider	40
Coverage	30
Hot	3

Selectivity, a relative quantity, refers to the ability of a given classification to reduce the scope of the selective processing request. In terms of a search path, the aim is to find the shortest path. Selectivity is computed as the inverse of the number of records it isolates (i.e., how many are left to examine). Selectivity is analogous to entropy, the inverse of probability of occurrence of an event as used in information theory. It really says that the rarer the occurrence of an event (or a thing) the more valuable that event is in conveying information. When structuring a query, start the search with the classification which has the highest selectivity and then, having found all the records which satisfy the initial criteria, examine each in turn for concurrence with the remaining selection elements. (Note that if a Boolean request is structured, the OR requires that the shortest path be determined and applied to each subrequest which is connected by an OR).

UTILITY VERSUS SELECTIVITY

The problem of security from the standpoint of denying access has been discussed in previous sections. Here, it is addressed in terms of efficiency, both in terms of reducing the value of the entire information system and, as it increases, in terms of the number of accesses and amount of supplemental processing. It should be evident that any restriction of accessibility to data within the system reduces its usefulness. This reduction of value can be overt in the sense that the requested data are denied, or covert in that the user gets an answer; but it is incomplete or even in error because part of the data were unavailable. The security provided within each system must be evaluated carefully in terms of that system and its performance goals.

Security is achieved by absence of certain data within a file or by selectively denying access to certain users. Selective denial requires that an access list for each user must be maintained by the system. This list can be maintained at the level of user identification and can be called at the time a user "signs on." Each request by the user can then be validated by his authorization at the time the request is analyzed. In this case, extra processing is required to achieve security.

An alternative approach would establish an authority key (password) at the record level and require validation prior to access. This technique requires access to mass storage to validate authority to read the record.

SECTION 8

Examples of Data Base Design

This section is intended to illustrate, by example, the characteristics of actual data bases. Five different examples are chosen to emphasize the diversity in data bases.

- Manufacturing (parts explosion)
- Cost accounting and project control
- Technical report dissemination
- Order entry, sales, and inventory
- Banking

Each example was chosen to illustrate the design process described in the previous seven sections. While the basic consideration for selection was their logical properties, the relevant physical considerations are described.

The design of a data base results from the consideration of all the information properties and requirements of a system and its environment. As such, it must deal with the logical structure of the information to ensure that the system can cope with each possible situation and provide the data required by each of the processing elements. At the same time, it must balance the physical processing requirements imposed by

- Volume batch update
- Random update
- Periodic reporting
- Selective reporting
- Initial loading
- Data integrity and security
- Unanticipated query and browsing

Each of these types of processing favor different kinds of physical organization in order to minimize cost. The data base design must accommodate, simultaneously, all of these diverse and sometimes conflicting requirements. The examples, hopefully, will illustrate the approach used in five different cases.

MANUFACTURING SCHEDULE

The company is involved in the manufacture and distribution of a line of industrial products which are ordered through distributors in either very small (one or two) or very large (500 to 1000) quantities. The factory is scheduled once a month for a 4-month period. Because the end product is customized for every order (i.e., a basic model is ordered with a list of options), production is scheduled to achieve a desired stock level of subassemblies. Of the various methods used to schedule the production of any item, there are the following:

- Master schedule—build a certain number in a given time period regardless of demand.
- As-required schedule—build to a schedule plus demand.
- Build to demand.
- Build to an exponentially forecast level.

As with the design of any data base, the first objective is to define the basic information element(s) of the problem. In this case, it is a material item. A material item has certain properties, among them are the following:

- It has a unique identifier, its drawing number.
- It has a name.
- It may be either produced or purchased.
- It may use other material items.
- It may be used by other material items.
- It has a relative position, that is, level of assembly, with respect to all other material items.
- It has a cost and may require the use of people, machines, or time to produce it.

Material items are related to each other by the way they are combined to produce other items. This relationship is both qualitative (yes, it exists) and quantitative (how much of A is used to make B). The properties of an item are absolute; it does not matter how many other places it is used, it still retains its basic characteristics.

Two supplemental entities exist in this data base for certain of the material items. First, for all manufactured (as opposed to purchased) items, there is a **fab-schedule** record, which contains economic order quantity data, set-up and unit cost/time data, and so on. For certain items, either purchased or manufactured, there is a **forecast** which contains the historical and forecast usage data necessary to perform exponential forecasting for the item. The data base structure is shown in Figure 8-1.

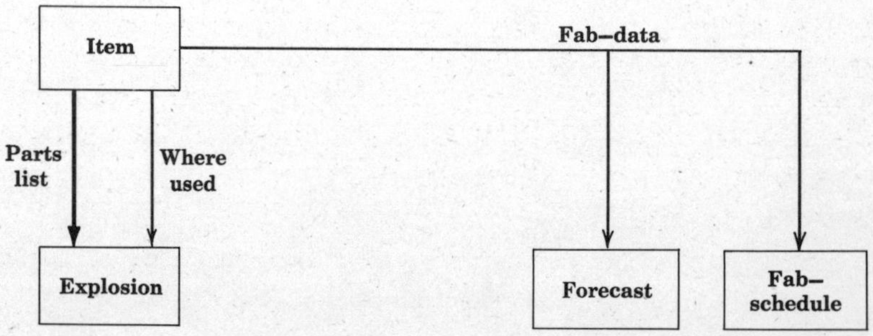

Figure 8-1 **A basic manufacturing data base for parts' explosion.**

In this particular file, there are approximately the following:

- 84,000 **items**
- 640,000 **explosions**
- 39,000 **fab-schedules**
- 24,000 **forecasts**

In any given month, 5000 **Items** appear on a gross requirements file (specifying forecast demand and desired levels). As the result of exploding the parts list of these 5000 items, 40,000 **items** or about 50 percent of the file is scheduled each month. These items involve seven levels of assembly. This particular data base is spread over three separate physical devices, each containing 7800 physical records.

The 84,000 **item** records are accessed by calculation based on drawing number. Calculation was selected rather than indexed sequential because of the following:

- Drawing number is unique.
- It was desired to distribute the data base as uniformly as possible over the file space.
- There is serial correlation in drawing numbers which leads to clusters of assemblies with large parts lists.
- The file is active with up to a 15 percent flow—namely, dropping old drawings and adding new ones.

The initial load of the data base was performed using a set of specially designed programs. These programs were written to take advantage of the unique situation which exists only at the time of an initial data base load. The decision to use a special set of programs is made on the basis that the cost to develop is less than the resulting savings over the cost of using the maintenance programs to perform the load. The load process consisted of the following sequence of operations:

- Precompute block number and sort the item records into block sequence, splitting the tape into three separate files corresponding to each physical device.
- Store the item related records on each device separately.
- Store explosion records.

In the process of storing the **explosion** or parts list records, 50,000 were found to be obsolete or duplicates (about 8% of the total). The presorting by physical record number resulted in the following:

- Ability to load with just one third of the physical space tied up
- 54,000 access versus 168,000 to store **material item, forecast,** and **fab-schedule** records
- 1.3 million accesses to store **explosion** records versus 2.5 million if presorting was not used

With the exception of the volume monthly scheduling run, all of the processing against this data base is random and replaces four existing sequential master files. The file is used not only by its owner Manufacturing but also by Engineering and Purchasing. The random processing uses either the maintenance program or a parameter-driven inquiry program. The monthly schedule run is handled as a sequential process. In this case, the highly structured data base is used to organize, maintain, and facilitate random processing and not as the processing file during scheduling.

COST ACCOUNTING

The process of general accounting has traditionally been viewed as sequential process with at least two master files, the Journal and the Ledger. The term "trial balance" may have been applied initially to the manual systems (green eye shades and scratchy quill pens) of seeing if the numbers looked all right; this may have been the origin of "juggling the books." As accounting was mechanized, the trial balance was the first shot at finding the bad data, since each journal will balance to zero if the data were entered correctly (debits always equal credits).

Double entry accounting is based upon the existence of two kinds of things, accounts and entries. These are related in two different ways; namely, a single entry represents a transfer of money from one account to another. The net of all the transactions against a single account is known as the balance. Because the term "negative balance" may incorrectly imply a "bad" condition, the accountant chooses to describe this net as either a debit or credit balance. Similarly, the transfer of money between accounts is handled as a debit and credit, rather than a plus and minus transaction. The two relationships between entries and accounts are then, debit and credit relationships. Specifically, two separate accounts must exist in order that an entry may be valid, an account which is being debited and an account which is being credited.

For purposes of convenience, entries have traditionally been "journalized." This is nothing more than the process of recording, in a book known as a journal, the supporting details of an entry. Normally, a separate journal is maintained for each kind of entry; for example, labor, travel and living, computer rental, and computer supplies. Using these three basic entities, the elements of a general accounting system are created.

The basic structure shown in Figure 8-2 was used by a consulting organization with about $1.5 million in sales and 60 employees. The system maintained 80 **journals** and 800 **accounts**. Typical monthly volume was about 2500 entries. In this example, the system was used for project cost accounting and billing details.

This accounting system preserves accurately the true double entry nature of contemporary accounting. Since an **entry**

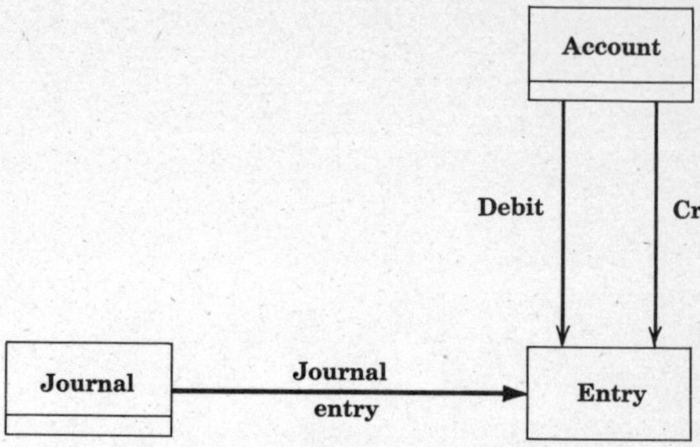

Figure 8-2 **Basic accounting structure.**

contains only a single monetary amount, there is never a question of sign. The balance of an account is determined by summing the debits and credits; that is, comparing the sums and computing the differences. As such, it is possible to determine an account balance at any time thereby facilitating the "closing." Furthermore there is no distinction between subledger and general ledger accounts and the Journals are always in balance.

For this implementation, the **journal** records are physically accessed using indexed sequential. The **entry** records are serially numbered within a journal (assigned by the system). The **account** records are physically accessible by both calculation (primary access) and by indexed sequential (secondary). The indexed sequential access of **account** records is logical rather than purely physical. Restart is provided by journalization of changes to physical records. Calculation rather than pure indexed sequential was selected for the **accounts** due to the expected increase in **accounts** (a typical new project would entail approximately seven new accounts to be entered). The method of assigning new account numbers encourages the use of calculation as a method of spreading the records across the physical file to facilitate access.

The full system incorporates three logically related data base segments. The first is the basic accounting structure shown previ-

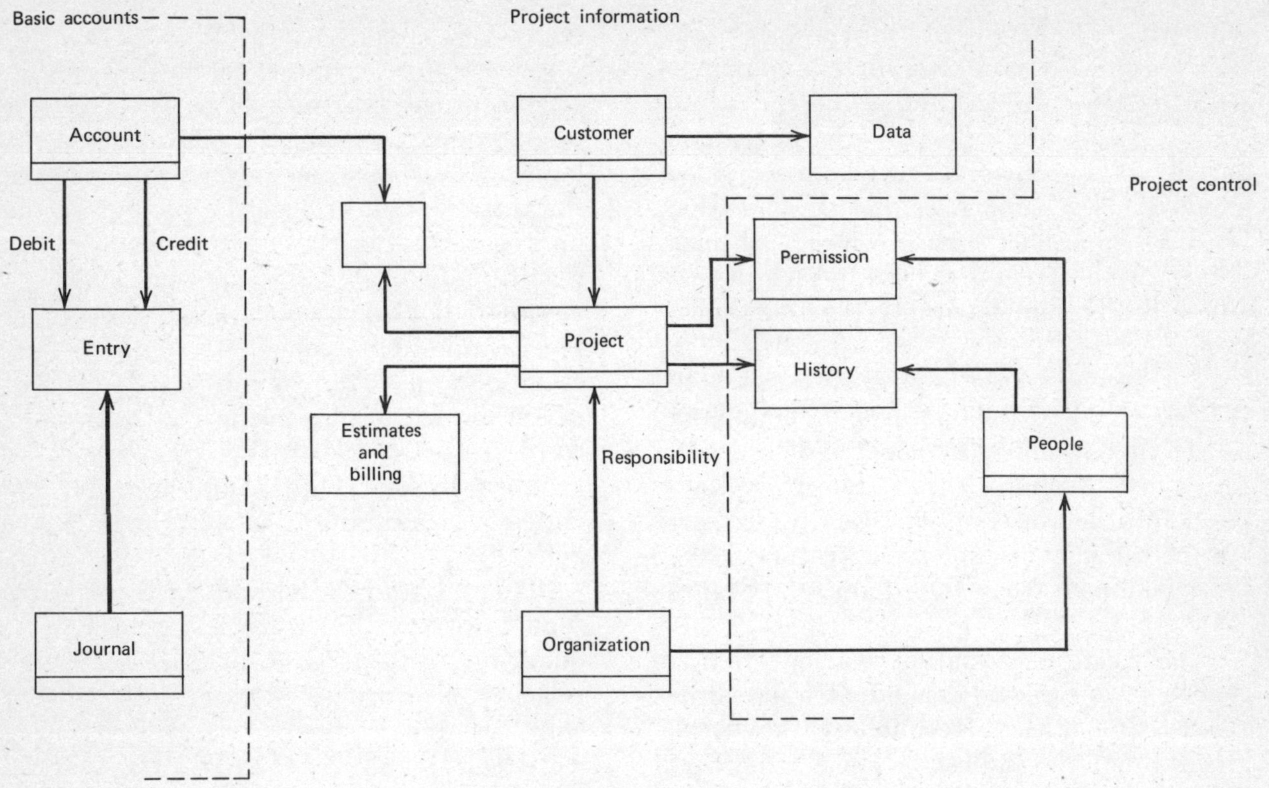

Figure 8-3 **Full project control system.**

ously in Figure 8-2, the second related to invoicing and project costs, the third used to control labor and material costs of projects and to provide an audit of these expenses. The full structure is shown in Figure 8-3, and was implemented in a 2 million character file.

The **project** record contains the basic project information. The billing instructions (fixed fee, installment, or per diem), tax rates, and so on are maintained in the **estimates** and **billings** records. These same records also contain sales and cost estimates for the project. The record between **project** and **account** establishes the variable relationship between these two kinds of entities —cost, cost reimbursement invoice, and sales.

The **project** control segment is established by adding the **people, history,** and **permission** record-types. Labor distribution is performed by **person.** A charge and, in some cases, per diem billing will be permitted against a specific project only if specific **permission** exists for the **person** on that **project.** Standard cost for labor is a property of the person while per diem billing rate is normally negotiated for each person on a job (at least for each labor class).

Since the permission to charge will vary over the life of the project, an actual history of labor by person and by project is maintained in the **history** record. In this case, weekly details are maintained for one month and then summarized. These data are used to report labor utilization by job and by person.

REPORT CLASSIFICATION

The Research Laboratories of a large corporation maintain a technical information distribution system for internal dissemination of current research information. This system is divided into two portions covering the initial selective dissemination and subsequent selective bibliographic search. The selective dissemination is handled by comparing the classification of each new report with the profile of each person. An abstract is mailed to each person whose profile matches the report classification.

The second phase is used to assist both the research and the operating functions in identifying technical documents of interest. This particular data base is relatively complex. In order to simplify description, several of the more complicated features have been dropped from the diagram (Figure 8-4).

The basic information element is the **report.** It is directly dependent upon three classes of entities (**technology, keyword,** and **author**) and indirectly upon two others (**key** and **component**). In other words, a report cannot exist in this system unless all three primary classifications exist simultaneously. The dependent records between **report** and **technology, report** and **author,** and **report** and **keyword** are used to accommodate secondary classifications. In the case of the **author,** it is used to accommodate any number of co-authors, while the other two cases are used to accommodate secondary classifications. Because of a historical use of **keywords** within the Laboratory, the keyword classification was maintained after the introduction of a more precise and less political classification of technology. As a result, note that keyword can have synonyms and also exist within a hierarchial tree; values for technology, on the other hand, have no synonyms. In order to facilitate browsing within the data base, the **keyword** records are further classified, or grouped, by **key.** This is nothing more than logically arranging the keywords alphabetically.

The secondary relationships between the **report, keyword,** and **technology** contain a quantitative value (zero to nine) which is a relative measure of significance. Specifically, a value of nine is assigned if the keyword (or technology) is highly descriptive with the value decreasing to zero for one which is related but of minor significance.

The secondary relationship between **author** and **component** is used to establish prior assignment to a **component.** The record contains the date that the person was reassigned. An alternative to such a structure is to include **component** assignments in

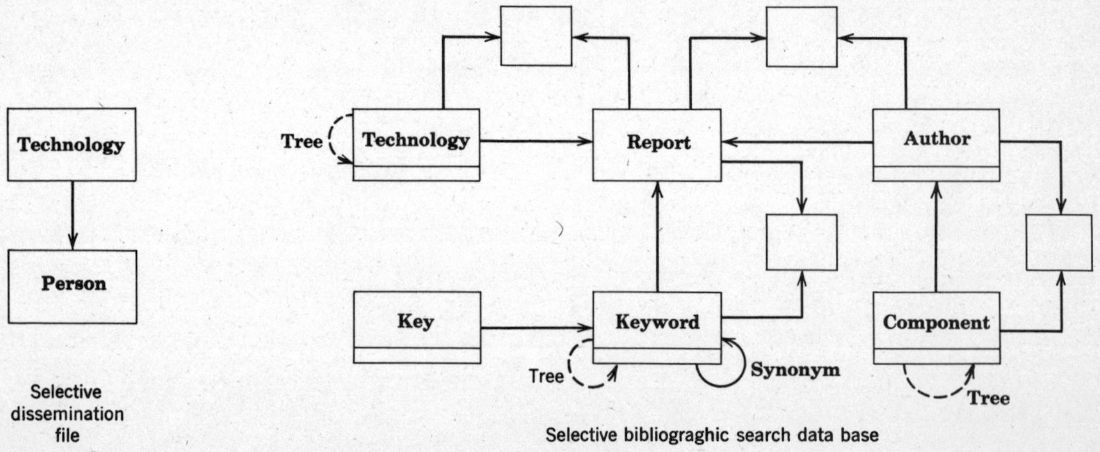

Figure 8-4 **Report classification.**

the **author** record. Such a compromise would, however, prevent the direct retrieval of **reports** by **component.** Such a request would require an exhaustive search of each of the **author** records.

This data base contains approximately 120 component records, 900 **author** records, 90 **technology** records, 26 **key** records, 400 **keyword** records, and about 2400 **report** records. The most active portion of the data base is the **report** section and its related secondary records. **Report** numbers are assigned sequentially and are independently accessible (indexed sequential) by report number. **Reports** are purged from the system after 5 years.

ORDER ENTRY AND INVENTORY

A medium sized company is engaged in the manufacture of a highly technical product line which is sold only to other industrial companies for use in their products. The product is extremely small and lightweight but of a relatively high value. The company maintains two manufacturing plants and carries inventory of finished goods in both plants and on consignment to its distributors and several of its larger customers. Because of the relatively high product value and the type of customer, it is necessary to achieve a delicate balance between the value of inventory and the time required to fill an order.

The number of products in the line is small, about 30, while the number of customers is large, about 1200. The system is intended to permit field inquiry of the sales data and order status, field entry of orders, and batch analysis of sales and inventory. The data base structure is shown in Figure 8-5.

The basic information element in this

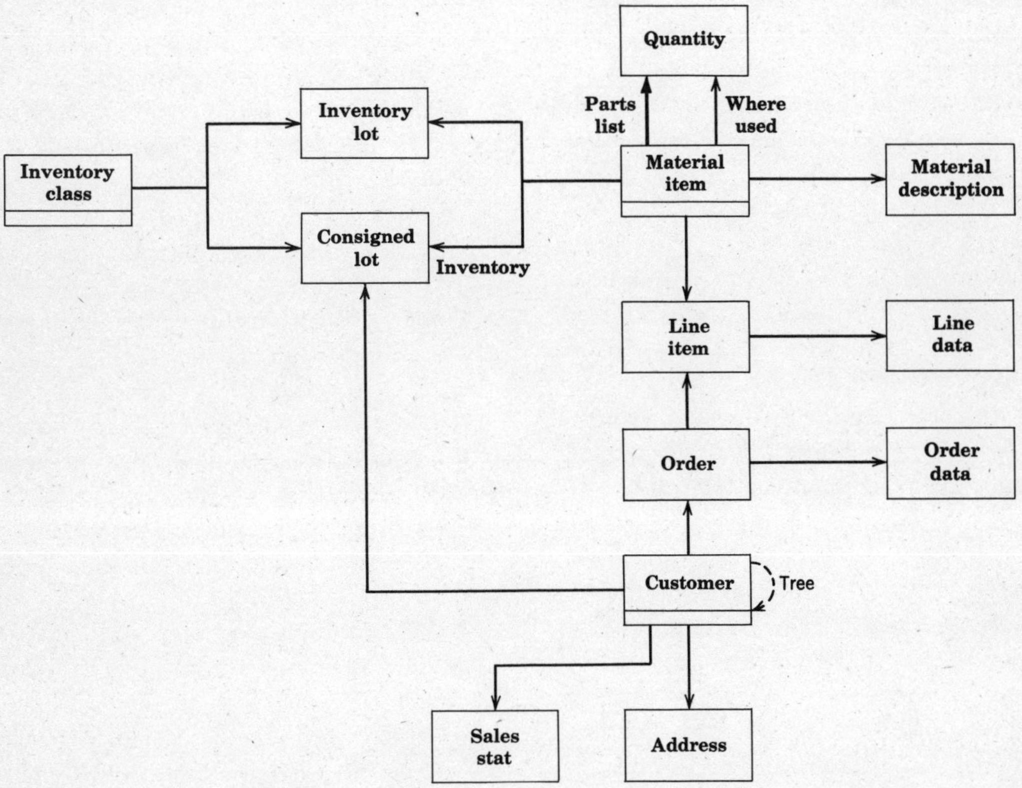

Figure 8-5 **Order, sales, and inventory data base.**

data base is the **material item.** It is independent of all other information in the data base; that is, it can exist without inventory or orders. Similarly, **inventory class** and **customer** can exist independently of all other information in the data base.

Material items are related to each other in terms of how they are combined in production; that is, as in a parts list and **where used** relationship. In this case, the relationship is quantitative in the sense that a certain amount; that is, how much is consumed or required. The **material description** includes manufacturing data, statistical usage data, and cost and price information.

Information concerning inventory is maintained solely through the use of the **inventory** and **consigned lot** records. Each lot record is serially numbered, within **material item,** and contains date and quantity data. Neither of the two lot records can exist in the absence of either the **inventory** or the **material item.** The **consigned** lot also requires the existence of a **customer** to hold the consignment.

Customer records may be related to each other in a hierarchial tree. This occurs when it is necessary or desirable to maintain the individual identifiers of the divisions of a company and at the same time their common membership in the parent company. Each level may maintain its own sales data. In order to facilitate the use of multiple "ship to" and "bill to" addresses for a company (even on the same order), the **customer** serves as the owner of its own list of **address** records. Within any **order,** the reference to an address is by number referring to a specific **address** record.

The **order** record is uniquely identified and contains the data which are common to all **orders** and all **lines** within an **order.** These common data would include such things as tax, discounts, terms, and supplemental invoice data. The data which apply to an **order** in general but are selective both in occurrence and in volume are assigned to the **order data** record. In this case, the **order data** record is used to maintain export notice data, plus supplemental information which must be printed on the invoice.

The **line item** is serially numbered within each **order.** This method of structuring requires that the **material item** exist (be defined as a **material item** record in the data base) before the **line item** can be accepted. Each **line item** can be shipped to a different location through the use of the address record for each **customer.** The **line item** record also contains tax and discount information for each line item that will eventually appear on an invoice.

BANKING

The banking industry, while faced with many of the same problems which confront other industries, is perhaps more sensitive to the effects of delay in processing of information. Obviously, the liquidity of their product makes them more conspicuous as a possible target for fraudulent attention from their customers. They must be able to evaluate quickly the risks associated with a loan. If an overdraft occurs, the bank must decide whether to bounce the check or hold it until the customer has had an opportunity to cover it. In situations such as that imposed by the 1970 mail strike, the bank must be in a position to evaluate quickly and continuously all of the individual customer situations which arise, and, at the same time, be able to respond intelligently to its overall monetary needs and opportunities.

As the pace of commerce increases, it becomes necessary for banks to increase the variety of the types of service offered, and especially to increase the level and timeliness of its response. One result of the effort to respond has been the growth of branch banking. As the bank's operations became geographically distributed, the need for more timely and responsive information updating and retrieval became necessary. The growth, and resulting dependence on on-line banking systems, stimulated the use of the data base which responds to the on-line information needs of the bank and, simultaneously, provides a profile of each customer and of all its customers as a group.

The specific data base example was implemented and is being used by a financial computer center which services many banks and their branches on a statewide basis. The full structure diagram encompasses over 50 different kinds of entities. There are four basic kinds of entities in the data base:

- Informational entities—customer name, bank name, and so on
- Dynamic entities—account balance, and so on
- Action entities—stop payment, hold balance, and so on
- Transaction entities—close account, drop record, and so on

The informational entities, including loans, mortgages, trusts, savings, and demand deposits in addition to customers and banks are relatively stable with an average life measured in years. They are static in the sense that they exist, as records, in the data base even though their contents may change frequently.

The dynamic elements are accessed much more frequently than the static informational elements. This frequent access becomes an important physical consideration since they will be accessed in the on-line, random query mode during banking hours and in the sequential batch update mode during the off-hours.

The action entities are included as a compromise between the designer who is opposed to redundant data and the speed fanatic who uses redundancy to gain response. They are a compromise since they are used to indicate an event that could also be detected by an analysis of the data in the base. In a limited sense, the action entities are information rather than data since they are the result of analysis.

The last class of entity is used to record temporarily transactions which have been accepted but not yet processed. The processing is normally deferred until the close of banking and at that time batched with the other volume transactions. Such transactions are sufficiently important (such as closing an account, overdraft) to warrant maintenance in the on-line mode.

The particular data base to be discussed is organized into five logical subunits. This particular organization was selected from both logical and physical considerations. The grouping represents a convenient distribution to physical units and at the same time a capability to fail-soft. If a unit should fail, the security copy and the journalization file can be used to restore it quickly by using an on-line spare or by bumping a unit which has a lower priority. The five subunits of the data base, in decreasing order of priority, are the following:

- Action
- Demand deposits
- Saving/trusts
- Discount loans
- Mortgages

The five divisions are approximately equal in physical size. Due to the space required to draw the entire structure diagram, it is broken down into logical subunits. The connections are shown where they exist. The basic operating unit is Demand Deposit which also contains the customer data (name and address).

The Demand Deposit Segment (Figure

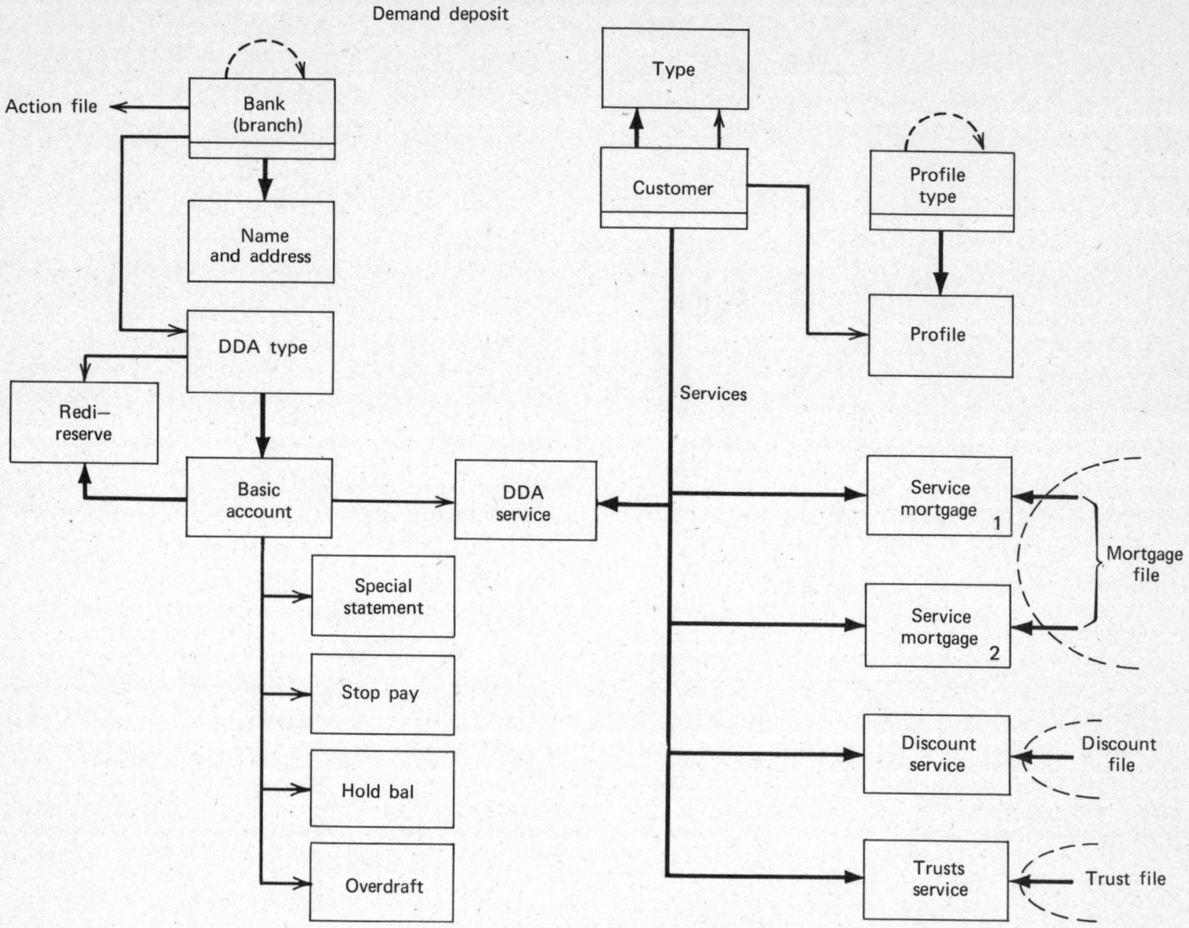

Figure 8-6 **Demand deposit and customer file.**

8-6) is the portion which experiences the highest activity and, with the exception of the action segment, is the most critical to the success of the on-line operations of the bank. As will be shown later, the Action segment is a condensation of the Demand Deposit Segment. The basic information element of the data base is the **customer.** A particular customer, person, or corporation can be associated with any one bank (or branch) in several capacities (individual, trustee, joint tenant, etc.) or with more than one bank or branch.

In order to fulfill their legal obligations, the bank must distinguish among each of the different possible roles of a customer. This is accomplished by the "name and address" record relating a **bank** and a **customer,** in addition to the distinct identity maintained by account number. **Customers** are also related to each other in the manner indicated above. This relationship is important to the bank in assessing the assets of a particular person or corporation and is of value in credit collection or estate settlement actions. Along these same lines, but for much more commercial reasons, each customer is assigned to one or more pre-established **profile** types. Typically these are age, residence, length in community, type of employer or profession, and so on. Such data are useful for promotional campaigns and customer credit information.

The **customer** serves as the "owner" of a

list which represents the bank's services used by each customer. In this case, two kinds of mortgage are offered in addition to demand deposit, discount loans, and trust services. These five entity types are used to indicate the existence of accounts and to create a linkage to the other three segments which are physically distributed over the other devices. These links are maintained with the customer segment since the customer and demand deposit segment has a higher priority than the other logical service segments. If one of the lower priority devices is "down," the details of the other service(s) may be unavailable but the knowledge that such service exists (and the account number) can be determined.

The highest priority segment of the data base is used to hold the action items. Each of the entities in this part of the file duplicates information which is also contained in some other portion of the data base. This structure is shown in Figure 8-7. As indicated earlier in this section, this segment of the data base is an insurance policy. It is the bank's insurance against the loss of the other physical mass storage devices. This portion of the data base is physically the smallest, and as such, is the easiest and quickest to restore. Because it is basically sequential, it is possible to split the action segment into its two natural parts and operate with each part on a separate tape transport if such drastic action were necessary (for example, a loss of controllers for mass storage). In the case of this specific implementation, the system resides on a drum which can also accommodate the Action segment of the data base.

The Action segment contains a record for each demand deposit account which has been identified for special attention. Because of the possibility of financial loss to the bank, it is imperative that the status of

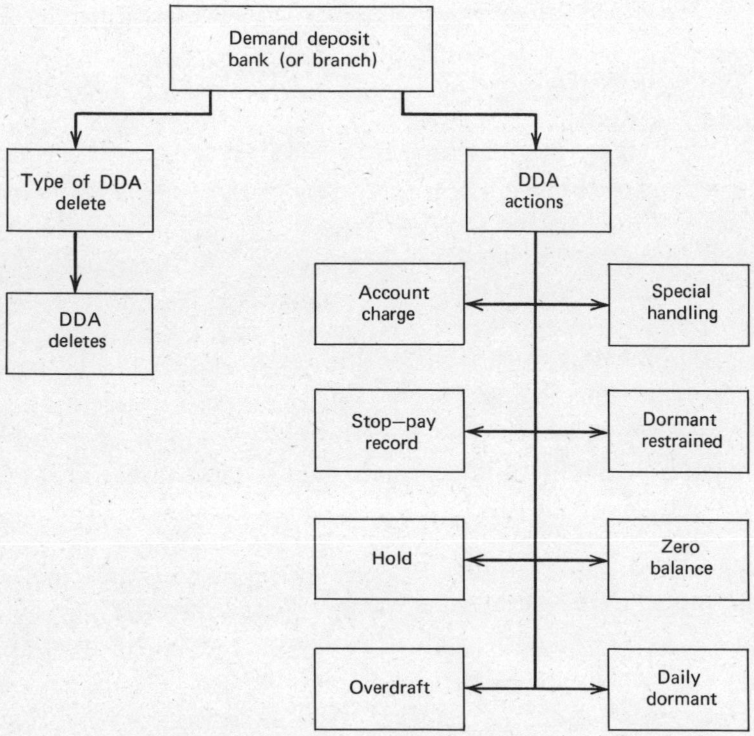

Figure 8-7 **Action segment of banking file.**

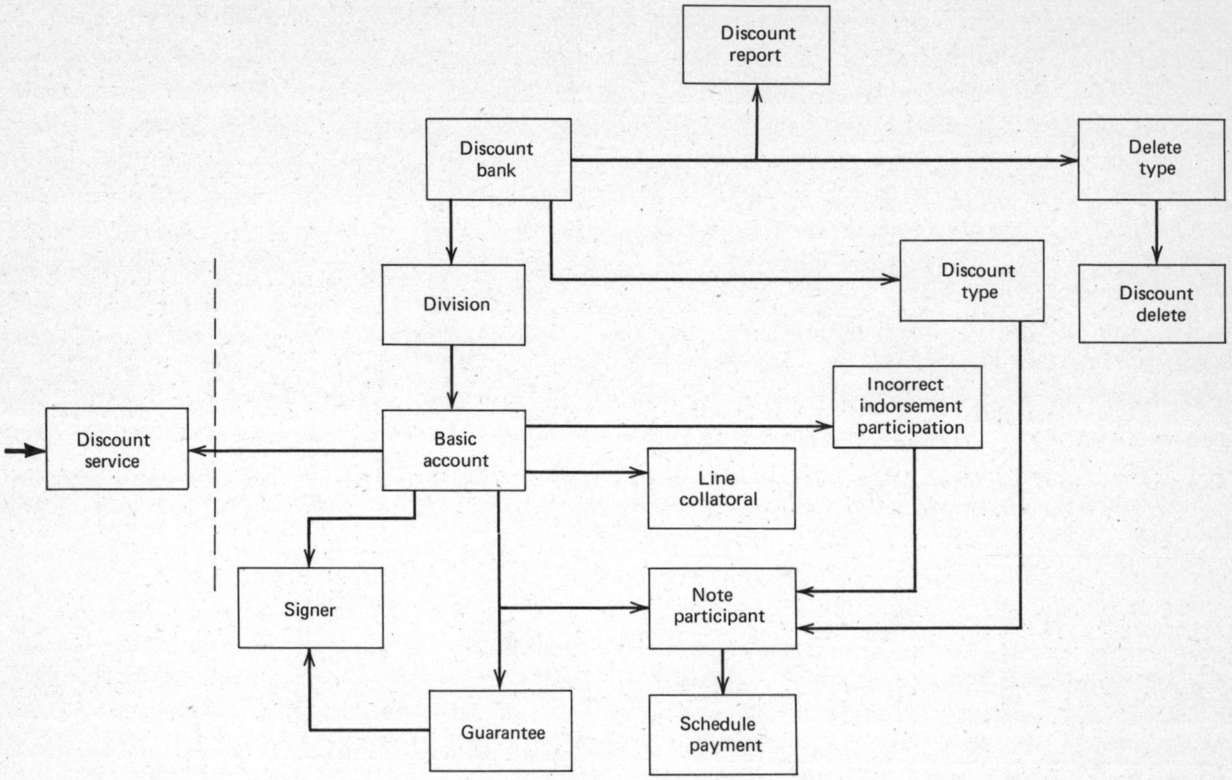

Figure 8-8 **Discount loan segment of banking data base.**

an account be immediately available to the bank management and/or tellers.

The third segment of the data base covers the area of discounted loans. This segment is linked logically and physically, to the customer data through the **discount service** record shown in the lower right-hand corner of Figure 8-7. This same record is shown in the upper left of Figure 8-8.

The discount loan segment serves to support the normal data processing of the discount loan function and at the same time to permit a rapid evaluation of loan applications. It is necessary, or at least desirable, to be aware of the total credit picture of a customer. Specifically, note the following:

- How many (and in what amount) outstanding loans does a customer have?
- What has been the customer's performance of payment on current and previous loans?
- Is the customer a cosigner on any loans and if so, for how much and what is the status of such loans?
- What is used for collateral?

In addition to such operational data, the classification by **discount type** and **division** permits a rapid selective analysis of the bank's outstanding loans.

The network which is formed by the **basic account, guarantee,** and **signer** records permits a single account to be secured by several guarantees. Each **guarantee** can in turn be committed by more than one signer.

The mortgage and investment segment of the data base is not discussed other than to note that it is structured to permit rapid access to the information which is uniquely related to mortgages and investments. While certain elements of the data base were not discussed or illustrated, such omissions were made simply to facilitate the description of the salient aspects of the implementation.

SYSTEM CONSIDERATIONS

A data base, as defined in the first section, is the foundation and the starting point for the production of information. The logical structure is created to aid the user, not to bind him to an untenable solution. In each of the previous examples, the physical structure was created to take advantage of the logical structure. As stated earlier, the kinds of processing which will be used to extract and maintain data within the data base environment indicate the desire to create more than one physical implementation of the same data base. This multiplicity of desired structure is commonly evidenced by multiple copies of the same file but in different sort sequences.

In more complicated cases, the form of the retrieval specification implies a desire to have a single copy of the file in more than one sequence. The fact that such a desire exists, and to the extent that it is sensible, indicates that the physical implementation should accurately reflect the logical structure. Furthermore, the physical structure should encourage such requests.

As the volume of data increases, the cost of batch retrieval increases to the point that it is economically worthwhile to create a temporary copy of the data base (or at least a portion of it) which is arranged (structured) to minimize processing cost. These temporary copies are a physical restructuring of the data base and not a logical restructuring. The most common use of temporary physical restructuring is in the production of periodic reports.

The main point of this argument is simple: use your head. Any data base should be capable of supporting more than a single method of physically accessing records. As in the cost accounting example, the primary method of accessing **account** records was by calculation. They were also accessible by the logical equivalent of indexed sequention. When **accounts** are accessed in collation sequence (for example, all cost accounts related to the same project) the processing is slower than if they had been stored in physical sequence. However, normal access during file maintenance, journal entry, and labor distribution is random and not sequential. As such, calculation is faster than sequential processing in the majority of cases.

Referring again to the accounting example; month-end processing is basically sequential with the same data combined in different sequences for reporting and analysis. In order to minimize the cost of month-end reporting, the required data are stripped from the random access device and reformated on tape. The data are removed in disk sequence thereby reducing the number of physical accesses. If necessary, or appropriate, it is possible (and often sensible) to create more than one sequential file during the stripping process. While the data on each tape are not a complete duplication, it is natural to expect certain key information to appear on more than one sequential file. Such selective extraction of data optimizes the reporting process.

SOFTWARE

Thus far only one brief mention has been made of the availability of software to implement the logical designs which have been discussed in the preceding sections. I believe that it is safe to state that software exists now for every major current product line offered by the leading vendors. In fact, most vendors provide more than one way to implement. The only basic distinction between these software offerings are the following:

- The ease in which the logical structure is transformed into code
- The computational and information processing capabilities of the host language(s) (Cobol, PL-1, Algol, Fortran, etc.)
- The flexibility of the data base verbs
- The ability to control record placement
- The ability to select one or more methods for record access
- The existence of utility functions to modify the size of the data base plus the ability to analyze the use and content of the data base
- Device independence
- Batch, remote access, and on-line inquiry/update capability
- The ease in adding or removing portions of the data base

It should be obvious that the list could continue almost indefinitely. In most cases a satisfactory level of data base software capability is available on the medium scale processors of all of the major vendors. Reduced capability (less automatic) versions are now appearing on the small machines (one is running in a 16K byte machine). For more detailed and current information on software offerings, contact your friendly equipment salesman. For example, the following:

· IBM	IMS/2
· Honeywell	IDS
· Burroughs	FORTE

Index